PASTORAL LIFE AND WORK TO-DAY

PASTORAL LIFE AND WORK TO-DAY

BY THE

Right Rev. J. A. KEMPTHORNE, D.D.

Lord Bishop of Lichfield

LONGMANS, GREEN AND CO.

39 PATERNOSTER ROW, LONDON, E.C. 4

FOURTH AVENUE AND 30TH STREET, NEW YORK

BOMBAY, CALCUTTA AND MADRAS

1919

PREFACE

THIS book, which owes its existence to the leisure of convalescence from illness, is not in any way original. It derives its best thoughts from the written or spoken words of many whom I gratefully recognise as my teachers. But my own experience as a parish priest in six different parishes is not so distant that I have forgotten its lessons, and my work as a bishop has already led me to treasure the knowledge which I have gained from many able and devoted priests in town and country.

It is impossible to acknowledge all my debts. The book was written out of reach of libraries, and may contain unconscious plagiarisms. I am specially conscious of help gained from Bishop Gott, " Parish Priest of the Town " ; the Archbishop of York, " The Opportunity of the Church of England " ; the Bishop of Manchester, " Pastors and Teachers " ; the Dean of Lichfield, " Pastoral Visitation " ; Mr. Walter Carey, "My Priesthood"; and the Reports of the five National Mission Committees.

It has been possible only to touch the fringe of a large subject. These chapters attempt to give some suggestions which may help the clergy to meet an overwhelming responsibility, and to respond to a unique opportunity. There is great need of a really

complete treatise on pastoral theology suited to the
demands of the present difficult but glorious day. At
least one volume of that treatise should be devoted
to the all-important, but too little studied, subject
of moral theology.

It is perhaps advisable to say that I have sometimes
used the word "Church" to denote the whole Christian
society, the company of those who in baptism have
put on Christ, the one family of God in this world
and in paradise which, in spite of its earthly divisions,
is still one family in the eyes of the God and Father
of us all, and may attain sooner than some of us dare
to hope to that oneness in body as well as in spirit
for which we are bound to labour and to pray. Sometimes I have applied the same word to that part of
the Christian society which we call the Church
of England, and it is hardly necessary to add that
I follow Bishop Creighton, Dr. Neville Figgis, and
others in believing that a portion of the Catholic
Church may be "national" without ceasing to be
catholic. But if, as is natural, I have dealt almost
exclusively with the pastoral life and work of our own
communion, I do not for a moment overlook the
great contributions which other communions have
made to the moral and spiritual life of the nation.

TABLE OF CONTENTS

CHAPTER I

INTRODUCTION

CHAPTER II

OUR AIM

vii

CHAPTER III

THE PRIEST

APPENDIX TO CHAPTER V

SOME EVANGELISTIC METHODS

CHAPTER VI

PREACHERS AND TEACHERS

Appendix to Chapter VI

SOME METHODS OF ADULT TEACHING

Chapter VII

HOLY BAPTISM AND CONFIRMATION

CHAPTER VIII

HOLY COMMUNION

CHAPTER IX

PERSONAL DEALING

Chapter XII

ORGANISATION OF A PARISH

Appendix to Chapter XII

A LIST OF POSSIBLE ORGANISATIONS IN PARISH AND DEANERY

CHAPTER XV

SELF-DISCIPLINE

CHAPTER XVI

THE DEVOTIONAL LIFE OF THE PRIEST

PASTORAL LIFE AND WORK TO-DAY

CHAPTER I

INTRODUCTION

THIS is a time of re-building, for the Church as well as for the nation. The Church cannot indeed lay any new foundation ("other foundation can no man lay than that which is laid "), but it is called on to test the superstructure, to remove what is unsound, to stablish what is strong, to strengthen what is weak, and to give a more careful eye, in future building, to the plan of the great Architect. In other words, we are bound to repent of our faults, to reconsider our ideals, to re-shape our methods, and to seek renewal of our spiritual life. The whole Church as the family of God, the army of the kingdom of heaven, is called on to make this venture, but it is evident that a special responsibility rests on those who have been ordained to be leaders in the spiritual war, messengers, watchmen, and stewards in the divine society. This book is a humble attempt to help them to think out afresh the principles of their witness and their work, in the light of the new conditions of this time.

The war found the Church, as it found the

nation, wholly unprepared. It took us some time
to get our bearings. It was indeed evident that
our national cause was right, and that we could
sound the popular call to patriotism with a good
conscience. It was clearly our duty to do our
best to strengthen the courage of the nation, to
provide for the spiritual needs of the fighting men,
to comfort those who were anxious or in trouble,
and to lead the people in prayer, remembering
that we were not claiming God on our side, but
asking Him to help us to be on His side and to
do His will.

But there were difficult problems to think out.
There were many Cassandras who told us that the
war was a proof of the bankruptcy of Christianity.
Mr. Chesterton gave his quite sufficient answer—" It
is not true that Christianity has been tried and
found wanting ; the truth is that Christianity has been
found difficult and has not been tried " ; but we still
felt that it was a strange reproach to us that nation-
ality should be a force so immeasurably stronger than
Christian fellowship, and we recognised that the
Church must bear at least some of the blame for the
fact that " Christianity had not been tried." As to
the justification of war, most of us saw clearly enough
that, while we are bound to work for the removal of
those evils in which wars have their source, and to
strive to bring about a better order in which God's
peace shall reign, yet in the world as it is we sometimes have to choose the lesser of two evils, so that
what is relatively right becomes God's will for us : we
were convinced that war was a lesser evil than
cowardice or treachery. But we could hardly doubt
that sin must lie at the door of so dreadful an alternative. It was indeed evident to us then, though it
is more conclusively evident now, that the war was
of Germany's making : we had laboured for peace,
and they had made them ready for battle. But as

Mr. Clutton Brock reminded us, "the Europe in which Germany became capable of this sin is the Europe of us all." And the Bishop of Oxford rightly taught us that the war is God's judgment on the nations— judgment, not punishment. God is not standing outside the world, hurling His punishments upon men, striking the innocent and the guilty: He simply lets us see what is the inevitable result of a civilisation which is largely based on selfishness, while all the time as the God of Love He is in our midst, "afflicted in our affliction," overruling the evil for good. We came under judgment not because, like Germany, we had exalted the nation above God and chosen national world-power for our supreme purpose: the trouble had rather been that we had drifted along without any clear purpose at all, and had trusted to a "progress" which left God out of the reckoning. Could God have been so ignored, could the selfish war-spirit have been so rampant within our national life, if the Church had given a more faithful witness?

Then we looked out on the revelation of our British manhood. There was nothing to be ashamed of here. Five million men—before conscription began—gave themselves to the country and its cause. Doubtless many different motives were at work. They were not a host of perfect saints, and they would be the last to lay claim to heroism. But they proved themselves to be heroes. Their courage, their dogged persistence, which not once nor twice brought us through a dangerous crisis, their good comradeship, their indomitable cheerfulness and humour, their readiness to do and suffer anything, proved the metal of which they were made. These virtues are good gifts of God, and the Church (using the word in its largest sense) had been among the influences which had produced them. But it was doubtful whether many of the men thought so. The "Student in Arms" and our chaplains told us (what many of us knew before) that few of the men were entirely irreligious, but that their religion was of an inarticulate sort. They admired qualities which are essentially Christian—courage, humility which will not brag, generous kindness, self-sacrifice—and yet were wholly unconscious that in Christ these virtues (with many others) are perfectly realised, and that from Him alone the power may be gained to achieve the very difficult task of practising them with consistency, and of attaining to our full manhood. The majority were indeed wholly ignorant of what Christianity means: they simply did not recognise it as a life and a power. Yet many of them had been in our schools and confirmation classes. Why had the Church been so ineffective in its teaching?

From our fighting men we turned to the people at home. Here there were some evil symptoms. There was a good deal of selfishness: not a few were making dirty gain out of the nation's need: there were some ugly outbreaks of sexual lust: and there were many who could not be brought to see that the goodness of our cause, and the sacrifices of our men, were a challenge to the nation to prove itself worthy. But on the whole the people had risen to a noble standard. There was a determination not only to win the war, but to secure true and worthy fruits of victory. Among the nations there must be a league of liberty and right; within the nation there must be a juster order, ruled by a spirit of common service instead of by greedy self-interest; personality must count for more than property; in the homes, in the towns and villages, conditions must be secured favourable to a full and healthy life; education must at last have its fair chance, and the children be trained not to be mere wealth-producers, but to be men and women capable of rendering good and happy service. What had the Church to say about these things? We were ready to do our utmost to further these ideals, but had we—as a society—really cared about them in the past? Anyhow, we were determined that while personal religion was as vital as ever, we must put God first, and claim the sovereignty of Christ, the Lord of righteousness and love, over the whole field of common life. Only through the FATHER of all could human brotherhood be secure: only through CHRIST could a power be found sufficient to meet the tremendous moral demands which must be satisfied before the better order could come in.

Thus with the consciousness of our shortcomings, and the resolute purpose to meet—as far as in us lay—the demands of a great time, the Church set about the "National Mission of Repentance and Hope." Of course we were misunderstood. It was said that we were bidding the nation repent of its part in the war, whereas—though we were surely prepared at all points to follow the guidance of the Holy Spirit—our consciences were perfectly clear about the rightness of our cause: only, in an earnest desire that we might be worthy of such a cause, we prayed for that gift of repentance which is no morbid melancholy, but the change of heart and outlook which comes from an honest facing of the facts before God, and enables us to stand upright on our feet. That was the *Repentance* which we sought; our *Hope* was for a better and happier England, an England which should have passed through the valley of decision, and dedicated itself to the Lord of all good life. And it was abundantly clear that judgment must begin with the house of God, and that the lessons of repentance and hope must first be learnt by the Church itself.

This national mission is not a spasmodic effort, but a sustained movement. The "message" in the autumn of 1916 was an important incident, but only an incident, in the mission. We hoped for "conversions" as the result of that message, but our purpose was rather to lead men to a fuller conception of what conversion means. It was no small matter that everywhere throughout the country the call sounded forth—"Seek ye first the kingdom of God and His righteousness": "let God, not self, be at the centre of your thought and your life—God in His splendour, His goodness, His love. Enter into new fellowship with Him, through Jesus Christ, and in Him with your brethren. Accept His sovereignty in every part of life: and under the sign of the Cross, and in the power of Christ's risen life, let the nation win victory in the spiritual war." Here surely was a motive and a cause worthy to enlist the splendid qualities manifested in the manhood and womanhood of the country.

The experience of the mission message in 1916 revealed both our strength and our weakness. It showed us latent resources of evangelistic power among our clergy and laity, and in particular most noteworthy prophetic gifts among many women. It was evident that there was great fire at the centre: the best people were more earnest about prayer and service. On the other hand, we became conscious of the grave limitations of our influence, and though there was a tendency in some quarters to "wear the white sheet of repentance with unbecoming ostentation," yet we came to understand what were the directions in which searching reform was needed. The archbishops wisely determined to appoint five committees to deal with the questions which had to be met if the Church was to do its duty to the nation more faithfully. The questions touch :—

1. Our Teaching. 2. Our Worship. 3. Our Evangelistic Work. 4. Hindrances and Abuses which Need to be Removed. 5. Our Witness on Social and Industrial Questions. To these must be added : 6. The Fulfilment of the Church's Mission Overseas.

The Reports of these committees are now published, and I venture to say that if their principles are followed, and their suggestions carried into effect, a new and happier chapter in the history of the Church of England may be opened, with the blessing of the Spirit of God.

Meanwhile there are signs that the leaven is at work. For example, the Life and Liberty movement is rightly claiming for the Church that freedom which a spiritual society ought to possess for the expression of its own life, and for the removal of abuses in government and administration which are an intolerable hindrance to our influence on the nation. Such freedom is already exercised by the Established Church of Scotland. And there is good hope that we may see before long a truly representative Church Assembly, through which the Church can make its living voice to be heard, and can exercise a real legislative and administrative power.

This is a question of machinery. Yet, as the chairman of the Life and Liberty movement has written, "the movement of the Spirit in the Church is grievously hampered to-day by the inadequate machinery through which alone the aspirations which He kindles in men's hearts can be realised in practical action.

"But," he adds (and the words are well worth quoting), "it is not the machinery that matters. Our hope is to see a Church which shall be in very truth the Body of Christ, strong to the fulfilment of His purpose, and supple to act as His organ in all the diverse and changing scenes of its activity. No longer a coterie of devout worshippers, turning aside from the world to refresh their souls in seclusion : no longer a congeries of sections and persons, with little of fellowship and common action ; but a force, various yet compact, rejoicing in its variety while united in its object, caring first not for its own conventions nor for the welfare of its members, but first and all the time for the kingdom of God on earth, and everywhere on earth; that is the Church we long for, the Church we hope yet to see."

Thus the heart-searchings of this troubled time have led to new possibilities of Christian work and witness. There is great hope of better things. The call to the Church is—"Hold fast and carry on." We who are ordained to be leaders in the spiritual war have need to reconsider our purpose, the meaning of our priesthood, the principles which underlie our ministry of word and sacraments, and the most effective methods of translating those principles into action. There is need of renewal in our study of the faith, our self-discipline, and our devotion. The purpose of the present book is to attempt to give some little help in that reconsideration and renewal. Let the prayer of writer and of readers be "tot sint Tibi laudes, o bone Deus, quot literas scribam, quot verba legam."

CHAPTER II

OUR AIM

IN every undertaking, great or small, the first necessity is that we should know our aim and purpose.
"Know what you have to do and do it" was the
advice of a great artist. "Ars artium est regimen
animarum," and those who are called to practise that
art must be certain what they want to do. Pursuit
of a clear purpose is indeed a lesson which our
country has been painfully but surely learning.
Thousands of men and women have gained happiness in discovering a purpose worthy of their powers :
the whole nation has become nobler in so far as it has
given itself wholly to a great cause.

What is the Church's cause? Have all the
members of the Church—have all its ministers—a
clear idea of the end for which it was founded? The
definition of a certain politician, quoted by Mr. W.
Temple, has become classical : "A church is a
voluntary association of individuals who combine
together for the worship of God in their own interest."
It is to be feared that there are "churchmen" who
would be tolerably content with this description.
Yet could anything be further from the truth? The
Church is not a voluntary association, but the society
founded by Christ :[1] worship is indeed the breath of

---

[1] In one sense the Catholic Church is a continuation of the
Church of the old covenant. It is the "People of God." But
we may truly say that it was founded by Jesus Christ, inasmuch
as its relation to God, its inclusiveness, its world-wide purpose

its life, but "worship in our own interest!" Worship, as we know well enough, is for the honour of God, and its effect on ourselves is to fit us for His service and the good of our fellow-men. Yet there are many church people whose idea of the Church is frankly selfish; they think that it exists for their own "spiritual comfort"; and there are many more who talk about the "interests of the Church" as though it were a self-contained corporation, jealous of its own rights, and given over to its own selfish ends. The Church can have no selfish ends to serve. It finds itself when it loses itself in the purpose for which Christ founded it.

I. What is that purpose? If the Church is indeed the Body of Christ, the instrument through which He who is ever present in its midst continues His redeeming work, the answer is clear. The purpose of the Church is the end for which the Son of God came into the world. He has told us what it is. The FATHER has the first place in His purpose. "I have glorified Thee on the earth, having finished the work which Thou gavest Me to do": "My meat is to do the will of Him that sent Me and to finish His work." That is its Godward side; manward it is the giving of life. "I came that they may have life, and may have it abundantly." [1] Everything which belongs to the fulness of man's being, everything which brings him into correspondence with his environment, comes within the scope of that great saying. But seeing that the God in whom we live, and move, and have our being is the best and greatest part of our environment, life at its best is the knowledge of God, and

were now made known, while through the outpouring of the Holy Spirit, which was the sequel of the Incarnation, a new life and power came into the society, enabling it to be the instrument through which the incarnate Son of God might continue His work.

[1] St. John xvii. 4; iv. 34; x. 10.

fellowship with God.[1] To bring men into union with God—that is our Lord's supreme purpose : life and loving service are one, for God is love.

Our Lord knew what is the enemy of life. Union with God must be union of will with will : that strange disorder which we call sin is the assertion of man's will against God's : always and everywhere it is the negation of love ; its essence is selfishness, and the end of it is death, which is separation from the God of love. At the very heart, therefore, of our Lord's purpose is the redemption of man from evil. He hates the evil with a deadly hatred : "in righteousness He doth judge and make war,"[2] and there is no truce in that campaign till the enemy is put under His feet. As for His brethren, whom that enemy has scattered and enslaved, His one desire is "to seek and save that which is lost," and to restore them to perfect freedom. To that end He came into the world ; to that end He died and rose again.

This great purpose is one. God is glorified and His will is done, when His children are in fellowship with Him, when from the far country they come home to Him, and find their true life in His love.

St. John tells us what are the means which our Lord used towards this end : "Grace and truth came through JESUS CHRIST."[3] He came to bring us the truth ; in Him we see the splendour of God, in His kingly majesty, His goodness, His wisdom, His love ; in Him we see also the real character of human nature. He came to bring us grace—which is the freely-given life and power of God communicated to the heart of man. The truth tells us what sort of God it is to whose fellowship we aspire : the grace gives us that cleansing and liberation and strength whereby we rise out of the old bad self

---

[1] St. John xvii. 3.   [2] Rev. xix. 11.

[3] St. John i. 17.

and find our true selves in union with God. Fellowship with Him must needs mean fellowship with our brethren ; the essence of it is love, and love is service.

II. Perhaps I have been too bold in attempting to express in a few brief sentences a subject so inconceivably great as the purpose of the Incarnation. But without such an attempt one must certainly fail in trying to define the purpose of the Church. For the Church can only do what its ever-present Head chooses to accomplish through it, and His purpose is the same to-day as in the yesterday of His life on earth, and will ever be the same in the to-morrow of (God grant it may be) a united Christendom and a better world.

God's glory and God's will—that must ever come first. To these we add God's kingdom, for the end which our Lord Himself laid before His disciples was "Seek ye first the kingdom of God and His righteousness." Ideally the Church is co-extensive with that kingdom : and the day will come when the ideal will be realised. What of the present position ? Shall we say that the Church is the army which fights to establish God's sovereignty, the brotherhood which unites in happy fellowship the subjects of the great King ? Even that, alas ! is an unrealised ideal, but we must not rest day or night till it is an accomplished fact.

> "And was the holy Lamb of God
>   On England's pleasant pastures seen ?
> And did the Countenance Divine
>   Shine forth upon our clouded hills ?
> And was Jerusalem builded here,
>   Among these dark Satanic mills ? "

But our ideal is not limited to England, or even to the greater England. The Catholic Church must work and pray till all the nations bring their honour and glory into the city of God.

And the life of men must be the Church's first

concern. The Church is not detached from human interests; it seeks to make human life at every point healthy, happy, and strong; but it knows that such health and happiness and strength are unattainable without the knowledge of God's love, and apart from fellowship with Him. Therefore its principal business is conversion, the bringing men into union with God and into active co-operation with His purpose of love to the world. If the Church is not out to seek and to save, it is faithless to Christ.

Again, as our Lord made war on that selfishness and self-will which form the one bar to fellowship with God and fellowship among men, so the Church must be an army which is never on a peace footing. As we consider this side of the Church's purpose, and look at our own record, "boasting is excluded." We have fought intermittently, and with very poor strategy, against some of the grosser evils—drunkenness, impurity, and the like. But what about the hardness of heart and the harshness of judgment, the unreality and the self-complacency which met with our Lord's severest judgments? And what sort of fight have we put up against the selfishness, and the covetousness, and the false estimate of values, which lie at the root of the injustice of our present social system, with its glaring contrasts of luxury and squalor, its slums, and its waste of children's lives? Here we must confess that if we have not forgotten our aim, we have been very feeble in the pursuit of it.

If the Church has fallen short it is not for lack of sufficient means to attain the end. The grace and truth which our Lord came to bring are inexhaustible. It was, we believe it still is, His intention to entrust those gifts to the stewardship of His Church.[1] The Truth which He taught might have been left by Him

---

[1] See Dean Church, "Oxford House Papers," Series II.

to take its chance among the many interests and opinions which compete for men's attention : the life and power of His Grace might have been granted separately to individual men, just as a crowd of strangers may draw water from the same fountain. But that was not His method. He formed His disciples into the brotherhood of a society, to which He entrusted His treasures of truth and power. From the first, the business of the Church has been to teach the truth and to minister the sacraments of grace. Of course there are no limits to the illumination, or to the enabling and cleansing influence, of the Holy Spirit. But to the Church, unworthy as it has often proved itself to be, and miserably divided as it is now, the sacred charge has been given, and we are sure that our Lord is still present in His Church to fulfil His purpose of life and love.

III. If such be the purpose which our Lord set Himself and lays upon His Church, how tremendous is the burden which rests on those whom He calls and commissions, not indeed to be "lords over the heritage," but to be leaders in His army, " messengers, watchmen, and stewards," who bear a special responsibility for the ministry of word and sacrament. How imperative it is for us to keep the aim constantly in view.

It is difficult to believe that there ever was a time when men "went into the Church" (as they called it) to seek a haven of gentlemanly ease. Even if the worldly advantages of the ministry were considerable, and "livings" were sufficient to live on, it is hardly conceivable that men should now seek such an office from motives of personal ambition. Doubtless, though we have got beyond the clerical ideals which we find (for instance) in Miss Austen's novels, we still have to be on our guard against the temptations of worldliness. They come in a hundred different forms.

Our chief danger, however, is more subtle. It is fatally easy to lose power and grace in our ministry, because we allow ourselves to forget the end in the means. How often we fail because we have not thought the question out, or have become content with some conventional or merely traditional standard. Here, for example, is a man who is contented because he has a communicants' roll of 400 in a parish of 10,000; he may indeed thank God for his little flock, and they may be a splendid instrument for the conversion of his parish; but "bringing people to their communions" is a means which requires very careful handling: it is not the end. Here is another who secretly thinks of his parish as the last word in effective organisation; forgetting that, as a means, machinery is indispensable, but that if it becomes the end it will throttle the life of priest and people. Here is a third who is an ardent partisan. He is convinced that "evangelical simplicity," or "Catholic truth and order," or "liberal thought" is the supreme need of the Church. His chief interests lie in that direction; all his reading is on those lines; and whether he knows it or not, his aim and purpose become cramped and distorted. It is right that a man should contend earnestly for the truth as he sees it. It is not given to all men to see that the Church is both evangelical and catholic, and the home of reasoned liberty. But the spirit of partisanship is dangerous, not only because it seems to admit of very strange standards of truth and charity, but also because it fatally confounds the means with the end.

There is another position which is yet more disastrous. There are some priests who drift along without any clear purpose at all; they are content to be respectable clergy, doing the minimum of "duty" which is required of them, sadly plodding along like a horse between the shafts; but no one can think of them—they cannot possibly think of themselves—as leaders in a spiritual war. Perhaps their training was defective, and a right ideal was never set before them. More likely they have become discouraged and disheartened by the overwhelming task laid upon them. In either case they deserve compassion rather than condemnation, and the whole Church is to blame for its lack of prayer and sympathy. Not one of them is outside the life-giving power of the Spirit of Hope.

Even the most faithful priest needs to remind himself of his true aim. We know what it is; "it is enough for the disciple that he be as his Master." Following at an infinite distance, we also seek to glorify God and fulfil His will by bringing His children to that fellowship with Him which is life indeed. We also have to make war on the evil which separates them from Him. To us He has entrusted the treasures of His truth and grace. And "who is sufficient for these things"? We know that our only sufficiency is of God.

CHAPTER III

THE MINISTRY OF THE PRIEST

IT is evident from what we have said about our *end*, and the "grace and truth" which are the *means* of attaining it, that the Christian religion is not a discovery which we make for ourselves of certain probable truths about God, nor a series of maxims laying down a programme of decent behaviour. It is a way, a truth, and a life. The way shows us God's purpose: the truth is God's revelation of Himself: the life is a God-given power for the fulfilment of a God-proclaimed ideal. As Christians we believe that God has made His name known to us, and has communicated His life to us, in and through His eternal Son. He is the mediator, the way, the truth, and the life: "No man," He said, "cometh unto the FATHER but by Me." [1]

I. In other words, Christianity is a priestly religion, for mediation implies priesthood. The one ideal—the true and perfect norm—of priesthood is to be found in the one mediator, "the high priest of our profession," Jesus Christ. How strange it is that when men talk about "sacerdotalism" their notion of priesthood should be based on the "sacerdotes" of heathen religions, or (at best) on the Jewish hierarchy which gave a shadow of things to come. The sacerdotalism of the Christian religion rests wholly and absolutely on the priesthood of our Lord.

[1] St. John xiv. 6.

Three notes may be discerned in that priesthood:
He is chosen and commissioned by God: He represents men before God: He ministers God's gifts to men. If ever there was antagonism between prophecy and priesthood, there is now perfect harmony: as prophet He declares God's will, as priest He restores us to the fellowship with God which our past self-will has interrupted, and gives us the power of renewal, whereby we may follow and obey the law of liberty and love.

Where priesthood is, there also is sacrifice. St. Augustine well defines sacrifice as "any act whereby man is brought into fellowship with God." That sacrifice ought to be sheer joy and perfect bliss. "Sacrifice is essentially the response of love to love, of the Son to the Father, the rendering to God in grateful use of that which has been received from Him. Language cannot offer a more impressive example of moral degeneration in words, than the popular connection of thoughts of loss and suffering with that which is a divine service." [1]

Does Bishop Westcott in those well-known words speak quite truly? Ideally, yes. But in this world as it is, the restoration of man in his folly and selfishness to God in His holiness and love must be a way of suffering. There cannot be sacrifice without pain and loss. Surely the experience of these hard years has shown us the redemptive power of blood willingly shed and of life freely given. Those sacrifices are a glorious reflection, yet after all a pale reflection, of the perfect sacrifice, the measure of the infinite love of God, which was consummated on Calvary.

In the sacrifice of the Cross our Lord's priesthood stands revealed. There, as the chosen of God, He perfectly fulfils the divine will: there, as the Representative Man, He makes the offering of a complete obedience: there He opens for us the fountain of the

[1] Westcott, "Epistle to Hebrews, p. 281.

divine grace, " for, from the fountain opened on Calvary, all the resources which the Church can use for the healing and strengthening of mankind are consistently derived."

That one full, sufficient sacrifice for the sins of the whole world happened, as we know, at three o'clock on a Friday some 1890 years ago. Yet Calvary cannot be dated. Christ is " the Lamb slain before the foundation of the world." The atonement is an eternal fact. It is perhaps a crude way of stating our Lord's continual work to say that " He pleads before God the death once died." But we cannot find adequate words to express the abiding issues of His presence as our Representative, and the unceasing outflow of the wealth of His life-giving grace. Calvary cannot be repeated ; of course we cannot repeat that which is eternal. One thing is clear : " He abideth a priest continually " : " the priesthood which He hath is unchangeable." [1]

II. How then does our Priest carry on His atoning work in this world ? We cannot limit His generous gifts, but " the Church which is His body " [2] is the great sphere of His priesthood, and is therefore a priestly society through and through. All the members of it share its character. " Ye are a chosen generation," exclaims St. Peter, " a royal priesthood." [3] St. John raises the hymn of praise " to Him who loved us and loosed us from our sins by His own blood, and made us a kingdom, priests unto His God and Father." [4] We cannot insist too often or too strongly that the whole Church and every one who belongs to it has a real priesthood. The whole Church is chosen of God ; it is the people of God ordained to fulfil His purpose ; the whole Church should represent humanity before God, offering at

[1] Heb. vii. 24.
[2] Eph. i. 22, 23.
[3] 1 Pet. ii. 9.
[4] Rev. i. 5, 6 ; *cf.* v. 10.

every place and at every moment of time its intercession for a world which has lost its peace because
it has lost God ; the whole Church is bound to communicate to all mankind those gifts of truth and
grace which God has committed to it, not as a
private possession but as a sacred trust. As to the
offering of sacrifice — every prayer truly offered,
every act of unselfish service faithfully done, all the
heroism of all soldiers of Christ, look back to the
cross, and draw their inspiration from the Spirit of
our great High Priest. And there is one great
representative action in which all the worship and all
the work of the Church find their heart and centre:
it is in the Eucharist that our Lord specially identifies
Himself with His faithful people, that in the power of
His life they may be enabled to offer those prayers
and acts of helpful service whereby they may be
proved to be the light of the world, the salt which
shall preserve human life from corruption.

III. Is there any room then for a ministerial
priesthood? How can we justify the words of the
Ordinal, "receive the Holy Ghost for the office and
work of a priest in the Church of God committed
unto thee by the imposition of our hands. Whose
sins thou dost forgive they are forgiven, and whose
sins thou dost retain they are retained, and be thou a
faithful dispenser of the Word of God and of His holy
Sacraments in the name of the Father, and of the Son,
and of the Holy Ghost"? There is nothing here
which contradicts the truth of the unique priesthood
of the one Mediator, or the priestly functions of the
whole Christian society. The Church is a kingdom of
priests, not a disorderly mob: it is a body, not a
mere concourse of atoms. In the kingdom there are
orders of service: in the body there are members
each of which must fulfil its own proper work. There
are degrees of priestly vocation, and in the body
of the Church the ministerial priesthood is, as it

were, the voice which pleads, the hand which dis-
tributes. The three requirements of priesthood—the
divine call and commission, the representation of
man before God, the ministry of the divine gifts to
men—are clearly fulfilled. A man must be sure of
his vocation, and must receive his commission from
those who have authority to bestow it in Christ's
name, before he can dare to enter on a position of
such tremendous responsibility. It is the position
of a representative man : as Aaron bore on his breast-
plate the names of the tribes of the children of Israel,
so the priest must bear before God in constant
supplication the flock committed to him, joining his
prayers in all humility with the unceasing intercession
of the great High Priest. It is also the work of
ministering God's gifts : he blesses the people in
Christ's name ; he is the minister of reconciliation,
bringing God's children to Him in holy baptism,
while to those who have sinned after baptism, being
penitent, " he declares and pronounces the absolution
and remission of their sins." Above all in the sacrament of the Holy Communion he stands before
the people as their representative pleading the
perfect sacrifice ; and through his ministry the one
High Priest consecrates His gifts, that He may, by
their means, give to His faithful people the treasures
of His sacred humanity and the power of His life.

In the celebration of the holy Eucharist the office
of the ministerial priest reaches its highest summit of
glorious yet fearful responsibility. But it is a mistake
to limit the conception of sacrifice to the ministry of
the Eucharist, just as it is a mistake to confine the
" ministry of reconciliation " to baptism or absolution.
Always and everywhere he is to be employed in the
great business of winning men to God ; always and
everywhere in his pastoral work of preaching and
teaching (wherein " the priest's lips must keep knowledge ") or shepherding the children, or ministering to

the sick, or caring for the poor, or leading the Church's witness for justice, he is offering his sacrifice to God. Much of that sacrifice will be sheer joy, and the true priest (like Him, "who for the joy that was set before Him endured the Cross")[1] will always be happy. But sooner or later it will have in it the elements of pain : those who are called to work among the heathen overseas have a big share of suffering, though they are gloriously unmindful of it ; even in a town or village at home a priest has times of disappointment and misunderstanding and weariness, which will never depress his spirit or beguile him into the folly of posing as a martyr, but which may in some small measure introduce him to the "fellowship of His sufferings" Who made the great sacrifice for us all.

IV. In all this description of priesthood I have tried to be uncontroversial, and I cherish the hope that I have said little which could offend any of my brethren. But one knows well enough that this chapter leads us into troubled waters, and it may be worth while to consider the causes of the strong antipathy which is felt by many minds towards "sacerdotalism." Sometimes, indeed, that word is a mere partisan label, a stick for beating an objectionable dog, just as in another line of thought "socialism" is, or used to be, a title of opprobrium. Often it is the result of sheer misunderstanding. But this objection to the claims of priesthood may sometimes arise from an honourable jealousy for real and valuable truths which, it is apprehended, may be forgotten or overlaid : the wounds of a friend may be faithful if they save us from losing the proportion of faith.

(1) It is feared that we may forget the unique priesthood of our Lord, and substitute many mediators for the One who makes atonement. We who are called to the ministerial priesthood are guilty indeed

---

[1] Heb. xii. 2 ; *cf.* Moberly, "Ministerial Priesthood," p. 256 ff.

of a ruinously false sacerdotalism if we imagine that we are substitutes set to do the work of an absent Lord. On the contrary, we know that He is always present, always at work; we believe that, within the Church which is His Body, we are unworthy instruments, whom He uses for His reconciling and life-giving work.

(2) Stress is rightly laid on the direct access of every soul to God through Jesus Christ, and exception is taken to any system which is supposed to place barriers between the soul and God. Our priesthood would stand condemned if it were a mere cloud standing between the children of men and the Sun of Righteousness; but we do not hinder any soul from any of those means of divine grace to which it is entitled; if we were so foolish or so wicked as to attempt it, God would give His grace to that soul without our aid. But those whom the one High Priest uses to minister His grace do not "stand between" Him and the souls who receive it, any more than the men whom He sends to give His message "stand between" Him and those who hear it. He does make use of human ministers, and yet (God forbid that we should deny it) there are times when directly and immediately He speaks to, and bestows His gifts on, those whom He has redeemed.

(3) It is sometimes imagined that the sacraments, with which priesthood is bound up, are a form of "magic." Something will be said about this in a later chapter. Here it is enough to point out that no instructed Christian man dares to imagine that the priest can make any sacrifice on his behalf which saves him from the need of making the offering of himself, or can bestow on him gifts and privileges to which his faith need make no response, or can propose to him some easy way of escaping the punishment of his sins while he still remains in them.

The sacraments are not mere *things*: they are the means of personal access with humility and trust to the person of our one Mediator.

V. The rest of this book is an attempt to set forth some of the features of priestly life and work. But it may not be amiss to close this chapter with some reflections on the character which every priest must bear.

(1) A priest cannot but magnify his office. To be called and commissioned by our Lord, to be closely associated with the redeeming work of Him who holds the seven stars in His right hand, is to receive a position of inconceivable dignity. The one thing which is impossible is to "stand on" that dignity, and to expect honour from men or to assert authority among them. If a priest is not humbled to the dust by the contrast between his own ignorance and weakness and the greatness of his work, he is unfit for his office. If it should happen that God has laid on him the burden of great and special gifts, he can only be safe in so far as he really knows that, while God is able to use such gifts, they are a curse and not a blessing unless they are dedicated to God in humble reliance on His grace. Whether his gifts be many or few he will not make the fatal mistake of imagining that he is indispensable to God. Provided that the work is done, it matters nothing who has the doing of it. We must be content to "decrease," so only that our Lord "increases."

(2) A priest is nothing if not a representative man. He must have a man's true quality before he can be a useful priest. If he is lacking in the ordinary virtues which men rightly look for among their fellows, piety and priestcraft will miss the mark. No doubt the priesthood is a profession with a science and art of its own: the minister of Christ must not be a futile amateur; yet it is even worse if he takes the airs and graces of professional dignity and merges

his manhood in the officialism of a clerical caste. If we think of the most devoted priests we have known, we shall find that, while there was no mistake about their priesthood, no one could doubt the quality of their manhood.

(3) With real manhood comes human sympathy. Was ever anyone more intensely human than our blessed Lord? Nothing human was alien to Him: He entered into everything human except sin—and sin is not really human: men and women of all sorts knew that He understood them and cared for all their interests. As the Epistle to the Hebrews puts it,[1] "We have not an high priest which cannot be touched with the feeling of our infirmities, but was in all points tempted like as we are, yet without sin."

So the most characteristic of priestly virtues is loving sympathy. There is no weakness in it; the priest will love his people far too well to make any compromise of principle. Yet the true priest will never be a hard rigorist, condemning the foolish and the sinful with harsh judgment. He will love his people more as he intercedes for them more, and the love for his brother whom he has seen will lead him on to an ever-deepening love of the Father Whom he has not seen, and Whom, with the flock entrusted to him, he desires to know and to obey.

[1] Heb. iv. 15 ; v. 1, 2.

CHAPTER IV

WORSHIP

IF our aim, as ministerial priests in the Church which is the Body of Christ, is that men should have life, and should have it abundantly, so that in happy fellowship they may co-operate with God in His purpose of love to the world, then it would seem natural to begin with the ministry of the word, which seeks to win men to God by declaring His good news; our first business is to convert, and in order to convert we must evangelise. Yet conversion is the work of the Holy Spirit: it is impossible without His grace, and that grace is normally given in the sacraments. The truth is that the ministry of the word is intertwined with the ministry of the sacraments: hard and fast lines of distinction may lead to bad theology. At all events, both have their part in the ministry of worship, and we cannot be far wrong in beginning with that aspect of our work which leads us most directly out of self towards God.

I. **What is Worship?**—What is worship? Shall we say that it is the highest form of prayer, or that it is prayer and something else besides? Prayer is the lifting up of the soul to God. A prayer which is "in Christ's name" begins not with self, but with God. But in worship the whole family of God, filled with the consciousness of our Lord's presence, and of His continual intercession, and moved by the indwelling of His Spirit, seeks to render to God most high the homage due to His name. Worship is essentially a

26

sacrifice, and the sacrifice of prayer and praise (the fruit of the lips) is hollow and unreal apart from the sacrifice of the whole man, or rather of the whole Christian family in which each man finds his fullest life, in humble purpose to do God's will ; and wherever that sacrifice is offered, the abiding power of the sacrifice of Christ can never be far away. Where this offering of worship is made, there is a sure inspiration for active service of God and our fellows.

II. **Causes of Neglect of Worship.**—Why is worship so commonly neglected ? Why do men and women not " come to church" ? The question rather is—Why should they come if they do not think of God as a FATHER who desires His children to be in fellowship with Him, or if they look on the Christian religion merely as a means whereby each man is to win security for his own individual soul ? A religion which is self-centred, not God-centred, can never find much room for worship.

The National Mission Report on the worship of the Church deals wisely with this question of the neglect of worship. It traces it to three causes :—

(1) *The lack of religious training in the education of the young.*—The Report rightly urges that, while it may be necessary to provide simpler services for the uninstructed, our business is to train all our people for fuller faith and worship : " it would be intolerable to deprive those who are capable of understanding such services of the training which leads up to them, and of the privilege and blessing of joining in them." In addition to full teaching on the week days, the Sunday School or Catechism will offer the surroundings in which the "balance can best be established between the three motives which underlie all such worship. There is first the sense of obligation to God and the Church not to be absent from the great assembly ; secondly, the sense of privilege in being admitted each one to his place in the court in attendance upon

the King; and thirdly, the joy that is found in its fulness in the presence of God."

(2) *The unsatisfactory position of the laity.*—The present condition of the laity is far from the New Testament ideal. The clergy have indeed a special gift for special functions, but the gift of the Holy Ghost is bestowed on all members of the Church, and while the main responsibility of direction must rest upon the priest, the laity should be regarded as partners in the ordering of the Church's worship. "In a society which is based on order rather than disorder, the functions entrusted to the officials (the clergy) cannot be performed by those to whom a specific gift for such functions is not given. But the Church is sure to lose in power and effectiveness if this distinction is carried beyond its proper point. The ideal of the Church, indeed, is still unchanged; but in practice the lay people fall very far short of obtaining that influence and effective power which they may fairly expect to possess."

(3) *The growth and character of the present industrial system.*—The Church of the early nineteenth century proved itself unable to cope with the masses of people whom the growth of modern industry gathered together. "Thus the tradition and habit of public worship were broken for millions who never recovered them either for themselves or their children."

"But, further, the nature of the industrial system thus developed, itself increases the evil. The persistent pressure of its competitive processes generated in the people a spirit and temper alien from the very nature of Christ's worship, which, in its turn, divorced from the bitter realities of the people's lives, began to assume in their eyes an artificial character. God became apparently more and more remote from the actualities of their existence, while the materialism which the industrial system engendered in the nation played havoc with those spiritual conceptions of life

which are vital to a consistent worship of God—
e.g., the idea of *fellowship*, which is an essential conception in that worship has been largely lost through
the individualism and antagonism of classes resulting
from the competitive system."

III. Thus the causes for the neglect of worship are
not entirely to be attributed to faults in the ordering
of our church services. Indeed we should be on the
wrong tack if we laid ourselves out for a merely
"popular" worship. There is simply no use for the
question, "How can we make our services so pleasant
and attractive that people will flock to them?" The
best worship will indeed never be dull or uninspiring.
But a cheap religion, which aims at being pleasant
and makes no demand on the worshipper, is a religion
which leads nowhere. It is quite another matter if
we ask, "How can we so order our worship that the
largest possible number of people, whether well or ill
instructed, can find in it a means of drawing near to
God, and giving Him their best?" That is a right
and reasonable inquiry, and we must try to answer it.
But the greater and better question is, "What sort of
worship is most in accordance with the mind of
God?" Such worship is sure to draw men to the
FATHER who understands their capacities and needs,
and, while it looks God-ward, will inspire them for
fellowship and service in the daily walks of life.

But have we any "pattern given us in the Mount"?
Certainly we shall find ourselves on very doubtful
ground if we attempt to argue that any particular
ceremonies or any details of worship are in themselves
specially pleasing to God. But the main principles of
worship are laid down for us in the Bible, commended
to us in the teaching and example of our Lord and His
apostles, and consecrated in the devotions of saints
and the experience of the whole Church. We must
draw near to God with boldness, yet in reverence and
godly fear. We must worship the Lord in the beauty

of holiness. We must put God's name, God's kingdom, God's will first. Our worship, as we have seen already, must be of the nature of sacrifice. We offer our prayers and praises; we offer what we have and what we are in living relation with the offering of the Captain of our salvation.

It is evident that these conditions of acceptable worship are most perfectly fulfilled in the holy Eucharist, the service which is our Lord's sacred legacy to His Church, and which has the sanction of His plain command. There we offer our fullest and most earnest intercession, and in company with all the host of heaven and all the saints we render our sacrifice of praise and thanksgiving: there we make the oblation of the material gifts which God has given us: there we " offer and present ourselves, our souls and bodies, to be a reasonable, holy, and lively sacrifice " to God: there, above all, with our one High Priest present in our midst we " plead the one true, pure, immortal sacrifice " while He gives Himself to be the very life and strength of our souls.

We can never rest content until all our people are willing and ready to worship God in that great service. How this can best be done is by no means a simple question. It is a truism to say that the service which our Lord ordained must be the chief service of the Lord's day. Wherever and whenever it is celebrated it cannot fail to be the chief service of the day. Our great desire must be, so to arrange our services that the largest possible number of our faithful people may, with willing minds and hearts duly prepared, be able to take part in Eucharistic worship.

There can be little doubt as to the ideal. It is that those who join in the offering should partake of the sacrament. Experience has shown that there are many parishes where the Eucharist may be celebrated at an hour not too early for those who are weary with the labours of the week, nor too late for the observance of the Church's ancient principle of fasting Communion. A Parish Communion at 9 or 9.30 has much to commend it, and we cannot but desire that all our communicants should be spiritually ready for weekly Communion. But it has to be confessed that many are not ready, and in large town parishes it would be impossible for all to make their Communion at the same hour. We are clearly led to the conclusion that in many churches there is good reason for a later celebration of the Eucharist at which many worshippers will not communicate.

I am anxious that this book should be free from controversy, and the question of "non-communicating attendance" is unhappily a question of controversy. But it always seems to me to be an infringement of Christian liberty to forbid regular communicants to attend a Eucharist at which they do not communicate. Experience does not give grounds for the fear that our people will come to regard attendance at the Eucharist as a substitute for receiving their Communion.

It is quite another question whether uninstructed worshippers, including many who have not been confirmed, should be encouraged to attend the Eucharist. I am not speaking of children : most of us would be agreed that, at least for some time before their confirmation and first communion, it is good for them to learn, by sight as well as by hearing, the beauty and greatness of the sacrament in which they desire soon to take their full part. But what about older persons who are only beginning to learn what worship means? The testimony of the army ought to help us here, but it gives an uncertain sound. On the one hand, a very keen and devout lay-officer told me of the lamentable irreverence which resulted from taking a battalion to their church parade at a very ornate sung Eucharist in a seaside church. On the other hand, there are chaplains who have found that, where the meaning of the service is carefully explained, the substitution of a simple Eucharist for the usual Matins has conduced to reverent worship, and to deep spiritual impressions on the hearts of many of the men.

This at least seems to be clear. Nothing can be worse than to dragoon people to this holy service against their will. Where the clergy are convinced that the habits and customs of a parish with regard to Sunday morning service ought to be changed, they will take the people fully into their confidence and wait until the worshippers are ready to accept a new order with convinced minds and consciences. There may indeed be some who resent the greater moral and spiritual demand which the Eucharist makes on them. But there may possibly be others whose consciences are really troubled at the change, and a true priest will sympathise with them and do all he can to help them.

We turn to other acts of worship. It is the greatest folly to attempt to heighten the importance of the Eucharist by disparaging the offices of Morning and Evening Prayer. One cannot but wonder which element is objected to by their detractors—Intercession or Psalmody, or the reading of Holy Scripture. There can be no doubt that there is great need for improvement in the Lectionary and in the choice of Psalms : such reform is happily in view. It is also greatly to be desired that, in order to adapt Matins to its proper position as an introduction to the Holy Eucharist, a shorter form of it (ending after the Benedictus) may be authorised. Even as things are, if Matins and Evensong are given a fair chance, they offer abundant opportunity for devout worship ; and there is good evidence that Evensong appeals to very many of our people. By giving those offices a " fair chance," I mean that the priest should take pains over the whole service, that the lessons should be audibly and intelligently read, that the Psalms and Canticles should not be spoilt by over-ambitious music, and that it should not be thought necessary to intone every part of the service : where intoning is considered necessary at least it should not begin before " O Lord, open Thou our lips," or continue after the third collect. To put the matter as gently as possible, decent reading and intoning are not the universal rule.

Perhaps at this point a plea may be forgiven for bestowing extreme care and reverence on the occasional offices of the Church : it is unnecessary to suggest that the greatest courtesy should be shown in welcoming and helping those who seldom visit the church at any other time, and in making it easy for them to take a real and intelligent part in the service.

What shall we say about non-prayer-book services ? Military chaplains, Church Army workers, and many others are urgent in calling for simpler services in which uninstructed folk, to whom much of the prayer-book is like a foreign language, can take a devout and intelligent part. From other directions the demand is heard for prayer meetings and intercession services, and other acts of devotion. What limits must be set to the satisfaction of this reasonable demand ? Clergy are plainly bound by the solemn undertaking given at their ordination—" In public prayer and administration of the sacraments I will use the form in the said Book (of Common Prayer) prescribed and none other, except so far as shall be ordered by lawful authority." " Lawful authority " must mean something more than the private judgment of an individual priest as to the prescriptions of " Catholic tradition " or " evangelical truth." There can be no doubt that the *jus liturgicum* confers certain authority on the bishop of the diocese, though there may be differences of opinion as to the rightful range of his powers. In any doubtful case the parish priest will be glad to shelter himself behind the responsibility of the bishop. Now I have no sort of right to speak for "the bishops," but I believe that they are anxious to encourage freedom of initiative in the effort to meet every kind of spiritual need. The danger of woodenness is greater than the danger of rashness. A bishop is, however, bound to require that these extra-prayer-book services should be in accordance with the spirit of our own Church. A devotion is not necessarily either good or bad because it finds favour with the Roman Church or with some Protestant communion. Our Church has certain lines of its own and they cover a very wide area; but a bishop is bound to order that devotions which travel beyond those lines must not be used in public services.

Moreover, I believe that "the bishops" would rightly hold that the prayer-book order must be carefully and loyally observed with regard to the Holy Communion and other prayer-book offices, with the exception of the prayers which follow the third collect at Matins and Evensong. But in other special services, which are kept distinct from the prayer-book offices, the greatest initiative, variety, and adaptability are surely to be commended. If a priest is a man of prayer, with a strong sense of reverence, he will not need a continual supply of "forms of prayer": it is not right that a priest should be ill at ease when parted from his printed forms: if our churches are to become schools of prayer we must qualify ourselves to be teachers of prayer.

Among plans and methods which have been found useful, the following may be mentioned: simple mission services such as are commonly used at parochial missions; litanies of intercession where there is some "form" as a general basis, but scope is given for special petitions; biddings to prayer where, after periods of silence, the intercessions and thanksgivings are summed up with a collect or a versicle and response; prayer meetings; fellowships of silence. There is no reason why the naves or aisles of our churches should not be used for these informal services, or why the faithful laity should not take their part in conducting them.

IV. Very few words need be said about the accessories of worship. In the God whom we worship, beauty, as well as truth and goodness, finds its highest perfection, and it is therefore right that we should do all in our power to make our worship beautiful. Every art may be consecrated to Him, and every art is at its best when it is dedicated to His service. Doubtless we can worship God acceptably in the barest and ugliest barn. St. Columba and St. Aidan offered their worship in a house of reeds and mud; only they took care that it should be better than the other huts which surrounded it. We also want to give our best for the House of God, and no one doubts that the noblest architecture should be devoted to His service. Is there any reason why the other arts which appeal to the eye should not be dedicated to Him and used in His worship? Why, for instance, should not the best artists in painting and carving, and metal work and needle work, make their contribution to God's house? Only, where symbolism is used, let us make sure that its meaning is true and that it can be understood by the people. And in every case let us be on our guard against debased and unworthy art. The best works of art are not always the most expensive. And it is better to have no adornment at all than that which is cheap and nasty.

Sometimes our conscience is uneasy when we compare the lavish expenditure devoted to the fabric of the church with the miserable pittance given to missionary work or the help of the poor. And we do well to be uneasy if the motive for the decoration of the church is our own glorification or mere human pleasure. But Mary of Bethany has taught us not to grudge money given for God's glory in ways that do not seem immediately "useful." We must beware of the fallacy of the limited-gifts-fund. There is no limit, except in human niggardliness, to that which may be given first for the work of spreading God's kingdom, and secondly for the glory of His house and the edifying of the worshippers.

There is another art which from the earliest times has been associated with the worship of God—the glorious art of music. Very much might be written on this subject. But, in my judgment, it would be impossible to improve on the wise counsel given in the recently published National Mission Report on the worship of the Church. Distinction is there rightly drawn between (*a*) *music in which the congregation takes part by listening only*, and (*b*) *congregational music in which the congregation takes an active part*. It is the greatest possible mistake to attempt music of the first kind in any but a few churches, where there are the resources for its proper performance. But "it is probable that those to whom music makes a most direct appeal, derive more definite religious impression and more benefit from music to which they only listen, than from music in which they take active part"; and such music should not be interrupted by the "casual carollings" of individuals in the Church. But in the vast majority of cases the singing should be of a congregational type. For such music there is obviously great value in a choir of men and boys (and why not women?) properly trained and looked after by clergy and organists, but there is every reason for encouraging the whole congregation to practise the music, perhaps in a quite informal manner.

But I will not attempt to epitomise the "Worship" report, which all ought to read. The only word which I desire to add is on the subject of the choice of hymns. It can hardly be denied that in all our hymn books there are many hymns which are totally unsuited for use in the worship of the Church. I do not refer to hymns which are bad poetry, or which contain bad theology (and such hymns are not uncommon), but to sacred verses of a purely subjective and emotional type which are very appropriate for private devotion, and may be of great use in mission services, but which cannot be sung with any reality on ordinary occasions. It is reasonable enough that our hymn books should contain them, for a hymn book may rightly be a compendium of sacred poetry for every sort of use, but it is to be feared that they are sometimes selected merely because they are set to popular tunes. It is greatly to be desired that we should have a larger choice of hymns which have less of self and more of God in them ; hymns of praise and adoration are only too rare.

Again we cannot help fearing that inadequate conceptions of the nature of God, revealed in Jesus Christ, may be due to some of the hymns which we teach our children. There is too much about the "mildness" of Jesus (He is "gentle," but can we call Him "mild"?) and not nearly enough about His glorious manhood and heroic courage. Indeed the whole question of our hymnology needs careful thinking out and drastic revision.

V. From the ceremonies of worship it is natural to turn to the home of worship, the house of prayer itself. Surely we have much to answer for in our treatment of many of our churches. It goes without saying that they should be treated with reverence.

Our Lord spoke of the Temple as " His Father's House," though He knew that the Most High dwelleth not in temples made with hands ; and His wrath was kindled against those who used it for base gains. But it is more likely to be treated with reverence if it is the familiar home of the people, used daily for Eucharist and prayer, entered freely at all times by God's children for devotion and holy thought, than if it is bolted and barred all the week, and opened only for two or three hours on a Sunday. One of Newman's beautiful sermons is entitled " The Church of God the Home of the Lonely " ; he is speaking of the Church as God's family, but the title should apply equally to the home in which that family draws near to the Father. It is far more likely that every home will be a place of prayer when the children and their parents love the Church as the Home in which the whole of God's family can find a place of peace and devotion.

We need not be above learning a lesson from other countries. Two memories come to my own mind. One is of the glorious Church of Monreale above Palermo, where one may frequently find little companies of men and women gathering together for prayer, without the aid of a priest : the prayers are led by one of themselves, a man or a woman, and it is evident that reverence has joined hands with reality. The other is of a little chapel on a mountain side in the Tyrol : we were starting very early for a climb in the company of two guides : as we passed the shrine the two men went aside into the chapel (where, by the by, the blessed Sacrament was not reserved) to say a prayer for God's blessing on themselves and us.

We shall have made many steps towards better worship when we have learnt to make the churches the spiritual homes of our people. Let us make a strong resolution that we will not rest until at all the services our people may sit, or rather kneel, where they wish ; that there shall be no more of the stiffness and starch of mere respectability, and that all our churches shall always be freely open so that they may become more and more " the House of God and the Gate of Heaven "

CHAPTER V

THE MINISTRY OF THE WORD—
EVANGELISTS

IN worship the Church lifts up its soul to God. A worshipping Church is a working Church, and the first work of the Church is to extend the kingdom of God. To lead men to the acknowledgment of God's sovereignty and to bring them into that fellowship with Him which is their true life, in order that they may fulfil His will and be His fellow-workers in loving service—that is the main business of the Church.

In other words, the Church is a missionary fellowship. "To preach the whole Gospel to the whole world is the whole business of the whole Church." Here surely is that great venture of the Kingdom which is the best "moral equivalent for war." The work of the evangelist is central and primary : whatever else is neglected this must be fulfilled. And the work is *one* in whatever part of the world it may be exercised.

The bands which make the whole world one become closer every year. That which is thought or done in India or China reacts on us in England. The wholesomeness of the best home life in England, as well as the poisonous growths which mar our civilisation, have their influence in the East. Moreover, just as the true nationalism seeks liberty for every nation to develop its capacities and resources that each may make its contribution to the good of all, so the true catholicism looks forward to every nation and race developing its highest gifts through the truth and grace of Jesus Christ, in order that it may bring its glory and honour into the kingdom of God. This cannot be accomplished without conversion, and conversion is the work of the evangelist.

We, then, who are called to be priests in the Church of God have our part in a world-wide work. We are officers in God's army, and we ought to be ready to go anywhere wherever we are wanted. The greatest scope for God's warfare is doubtless to be found overseas. Yet there ought to be nothing tame or uninspiring in the work of a mission priest in a big industrial parish, or indeed in a country village. In the priest's work anywhere there is a union of romance and reality : it is a great adventure. The one inexcusable thing is that we should forget our primary purpose. How can a man settle down to be a comfortable and conventional clergyman, contentedly feeding a few carefully chosen sheep, while there are hundreds who are "lost" because they have not found God? For very many of us there is no chance of leaving the ninety and nine while we seek the one sheep that is lost : our work is rather to seek the ninety and nine and bring them home to the Good Shepherd. To quote the National Mission's Evangelistic Report :—

" To evangelise is so to present Christ Jesus in the power of the Holy Spirit, that men shall come to put their trust in God through Him, to accept Him as their Saviour, to serve Him as their King in the fellowship of His Church."

I. Here, as elsewhere, our business is to lead. But the ministry of evangelism belongs to the whole Church, and not merely to the priesthood. This is true whether we look at the matter from the point of view of the individual or of the whole society.

(1) As the greatest obstacle to the acceptance of Christianity is the inconsistency of Christians, so the most convincing argument is the witness of a downright Christian life. No doubt those complaints of the sins of Christians which are familiar to every parish priest are sometimes unfair : there is a failure to distinguish between the hypocrisy of the self-satisfied Pharisees and the honest effort of the man who, amid many temptations, tries his best, and frequently fails, but ceases not to seek God's grace. But there are self-satisfied Pharisees and merely conventional Christians, and as they are the worst stumbling-block to the progress of the kingdom, so the unconscious testimony of the brave, faithful, loving Christian man is its most powerful aid. As one of the nonconformists who gave evidence before the National Mission Committee wisely said, if we could put a saint in every factory, and then, when there were enough to go round, a saint in every department and shop of every factory, we should make big strides towards the conversion of England. Therefore, if God deigns to use us for the making of saints, our work will not be in vain ; only let us be sure that they are saints, and not self-centred pious persons, who are only anxious about the comfort of their own souls.

(2) Yet something more is needed than the witness of individual Christians ; the whole Church as a body must commend the message which it brings. Here at once we are brought up against the mischief of a divided Christendom. The Church is not one body. The reproach of our divisions is always with us. We cannot heal by impatient nostrums the disease of centuries. But we can pray and work for unity, and as a first step we can put away from us the divisive temper, the bitter recriminations, the stupid refusal to understand the other Christian's standpoint, or to recognise the manifest fruits of the Spirit which God

has granted him. After all, it is not the fact that there are many "churches"—grievous as that is to the instructed Christian—but rather the bitter controversial spirit, which causes people to shake their heads at us and to prefer a vague and diffused Christianity to that gospel of life and power for which the whole Church ought to stand.

If there is a devil of division, he has a partner, the devil of unbrotherliness. If the Church were now, what it was once, a warm-hearted, loving brotherhood, it would soon be on the way to evangelise England. There are parishes where the Church comes near to that ideal, and they are centres of warmth where you will hear of conversions. But we find too frequently an aloofness, a respect for worn-out class distinctions, a chill disregard for a brother's good, which simply freeze the channels of divine grace.

When the Church has learnt the happy secret of brotherly fellowship among its own members, it will assuredly give a more faithful witness for righteousness and brotherhood in the common relationships between man and man, and when that witness is heard, men will listen to our message who are now deaf to it, because they will see that our creed is really translated into action. As things now stand, many men are saying, "You speak fair words about the brotherhood of man; but what have you done to promote that justice between man and man which is the condition of brotherly goodwill, or to lead men towards co-operation one with another in mutual service instead of their striving one against another for private gain? You have done much to relieve poverty, but have you really been at the head of every effort to prevent the degrading destitution, with its incidents of foul slums and sweated labour and wasted infant life, which dehumanises God's children, and is the deadly enemy of spiritual life?" We cannot plead "not guilty"—though there have been churchmen who have done their best. We can only resolve that we will do better; and let it be said with all the emphasis that we can command that we shall not strive after justice and brotherhood in order to seek popularity or to win the favour of democracy (God save us from such motives), but simply because this work is right, and is an important fruit of applied Christianity. Then we shall find that the witness of the Church is preparing the way for a full acceptance of the Gospel.[1]

II. The first condition of evangelism is a Church which, itself an example of warm and loving brotherliness, is a power that makes for brotherhood among men. But we cannot insist too often that those who are to live in brotherhood together must believe in the one FATHER, and we know that He is revealed to us in JESUS CHRIST. There must be a message: " How shall men hear without a preacher ? "

Who are to be the messengers ? In all ages of the Church's history there have been evangelists among the laity. Their aid was never more needed, and never more cordially to be welcomed, than to-day. And it is abundantly evident that the Holy Spirit has bestowed this gift on women as well as men. No problem is more urgent than that of training such evangelists (for even Spirit-inspired men and women need to stir up and cultivate their gift), and of finding the best opportunity and scope for their service. With regard to the evangelistic ministry of women, there may be some question as to the expediency of calling them to preach in our churches at this present time, but I can see no principle of Catholic order

---

[1] It should also be noted that abuses and injustices in our present system of church administration are a grave hindrance to evangelisation. " So long as the Church in her own life tolerates injustices and inequalities, and shrinks from the sacrifices which may be needed to end them, she is not likely to convince England that she is the divinely accredited representative of Christ."—" N.M. Report on Evangelistic Work," p. 38.

which forbids it. And after all, the opportunities of reaching those who are unhappily alienated from the Church are to be found outside our churches rather than within them. The message of the National Mission was often given most effectively in public halls or in the open air.

Let us by all means encourage our lay evangelists of both sexes to make full proof of their ministry. But the responsibility for the conversion of souls must rest in fullest measure on those who, at their ordination, were given a special authority to declare the divine message. Are all priests then bound to be evangelists? In a measure, yes; for all have to "seek for God's sheep who are scattered abroad." Any priest who never makes a direct effort to convert souls is untrue to his calling. But it is undoubtedly true that many good priests have not received that special spiritual gift which enables them to preach with convincing and converting power, though (on the other hand) the National Mission proved that many humble priests who had never been conscious of this gift found grace from God to equip them for their work. It is one of the "best gifts," and one which we may humbly pray God to give us. But there can be little doubt that we should be wise in taking a leaf out of the book of the Church in India, and in developing a special order of evangelists, who should supplement the regular pastoral work of the parish clergy.

III. It remains to consider evangelistic methods, and the nature of our message and our appeal. There is great need of constant freshness in initiating new methods; we can none of us be satisfied with the plans which we have followed, and the whole Church ought to wait upon the Holy Spirit that He may teach us what new departure He would have us make.[1]

[1] Some notes on evangelistic methods are given in the appendix to this chapter.

As to the message, we have to bring out of our treasures things new and old. We are not so foolish as to invent a new Gospel. The "old, old story of Jesus and His love," the message of the Cross, was never more needed than it is now.[1] Yet gospel means good *news*, and the water of life can never be stagnant. The old conventional language, even when it consists of such simple phrases as "coming to JESUS," or "finding CHRIST," is meaningless to many minds. And at this present time the great sacrifice of Him who gave His life for His friends must come home to the minds and consciences of many who thought little of it in the old easy days. Elaborate theories of the atonement are less wanted than ever : but, more than ever before, men need to be at one with a God whom Calvary proves to be the source of self-sacrificing love : more than ever before, the message of the power of the resurrection, and the ever present Spirit of love and of comfort, strikes the note to which troubled hearts are constrained to respond.

But I believe it would be true to say that the appeal to-day must be rather that of the crucified and risen Lord, who, as a heroic leader, calls us to follow Him, and as our Saviour makes us clean and free and fit for fellowship in His warfare, than of One who brings us a personal security and blessedness. God forbid that we should think lightly of those good things past men's understanding which He has prepared for those who love Him, or that we should ever forget how utter is our need of His saving help. But our present point is that, as we have learnt in the stress of war that the appeal to self-interest is nothing, and the appeal for self-sacrifice is everything, so in the witness and warfare for God's kingdom the call which brings out the best in men is the call to

[1] Most parish priests can testify to the supreme opportunities of Holy Week and Good Friday.

follow Him who gave Himself for us, and to venture everything in His service. It is an astonishing thing that God should call us into fellowship with Him as His co-workers: but if Christianity is true, it is certain that God wants us, and when men have once learnt His nature and character His appeal is irresistible. Only let it be remembered that they never will learn God's nature unless they have knowledge of Jesus Christ.

The new appeal which follows a fresh interpretation of old truths may be illustrated by two great words which are characteristic of the Gospel message— *Salvation* and *Conversion*.

"Salvation" is one of the master words of religion. It means a state of health, that condition of right moral and spiritual equilibrium which has its effect even on the body. The best thinkers of the Greek and Roman world believed that this *soteria* could only come from right relationship with God. Christianity did what paganism could never do. The Faith at once revealed the truth about God, and showed the way by which man could be made at one with Him; it is the way of the cross and resurrection of Jesus Christ. But is this well-being of the whole man, with the happiness that it brings, an end in itself? That is the crux of the position. Is self or is God to be the centre? We have surely been too ready to appeal to a selfish individualism. Certainly God's will is that we should "enjoy Him for ever"; but we are not therefore justified in appealing to the motive of a desire for personal security and happiness. God's will and God's kingdom are our end; He calls on us to co-operate with Him in His great purpose of love towards the world. But we can never do this unless we are in a "state of salvation," that moral and spiritual health which results from fellowship with Him. God's kingdom of love is the end; salvation is the necessary means.

"Conversion" is the action by which man is brought into salvation. It is the movement, sometimes sudden and catastrophic, sometimes gentle and gradual, like the turning of a flower to the sun, whereby man turns from darkness to light; it is the son's coming home to the father. In the current idea of conversion there have been two mistaken tendencies. First, we have been too ready to let men think that only sinners of the grosser sort, like drunkards and profligates, require conversion, whereas nothing can be clearer than that the hard-hearted, the unloving, the self-satisfied, and the covetous stand in even greater need of a complete change of heart and life. Secondly, conversion has often been associated with violent emotions, coupled perhaps with a most self-centred religious outlook ("that will be glory for me"); there may or may not be strong emotion when a man finds God, but the essence of conversion is in the will; it is the deliberate acceptance of God as King.

Thus the Gospel which brings men through conversion to salvation is the Gospel of the kingdom. It leads men to see and know Christ, so that in Him they may find that health and life and power which will enable them to follow Him and serve Him in the great venture of His kingdom. In Him they are to find peace, in order that under His banner they may make war.

IV. What, then, are the qualities required in an evangelist? To some extent they are those which every preacher and teacher ought to possess, and which will be considered in the next chapter. But—at the risk of repetition—we will briefly mention four conditions of an effective ministry of conversion.

(1) If we are to convert others we must be converted men ourselves. If we are to lead others to penitence we must ourselves be penitent. We must have determined to turn our backs on all unworthy motives, all selfishness and self-seeking, and to give

ourselves to Christ as King, for the work of His kingdom.

(2) We must be in close human touch with all around us. Our Lord was the friend of publicans and sinners; He had compassion on the multitude. We shall never convert our people if we are superior persons. We must understand their temptations with a real human sympathy.

(3) We must be ready to move out of old ruts and learn to be resourceful. We might use the pulpits of our churches more effectively than we sometimes do; but we must also get out into the open and buy up every sort of opportunity which God puts in our way. When St. Paul tells us "to be instant in season and out of season," he does not mean that it is our business obtrusively to "do good" to people on all occasions. But he does mean that we must be careful not to settle down into a conventional round of "clerical duty."

(4) I have spoken of "converting" people. But let us not forget that it is always the Holy Spirit that converts. An American evangelist is reported to have said to a parish priest, "If you will lend me your pulpit for a fortnight I will guarantee to make fifteen conversions every day." God save us from such a miserable travesty of the greatest work in the world. We can only say our "Veni Creator Spiritus," and humbly waiting on Him, offer ourselves to be used as and when He wills, and if we have the supreme privilege of bringing men to God, we shall give Him all the glory.

4

APPENDIX TO CHAPTER V

SOME EVANGELISTIC METHODS

1. **Parochial Missions.**—The method of a special evangelistic effort, under the guidance of an experienced missioner, and lasting for ten days or longer, is well known. It is probably not so effectual as it was forty years ago. But it is by no means "played out." The essentials are (*a*) the preparation of sustained and earnest prayer; (*b*) the choice of good missioners; (*c*) the concentration of every available worker in making the mission known in every corner of the parish; (*d*) the buying up of every possible opportunity for giving the message; (*e*) faithful following up.

Teaching missions are of great value. They are indirectly evangelistic, in so far as they equip the communicants to be good missionaries.

For Parochial Missions, see the Bishop of London, "Work in Great Cities" (Gardner, Barton & Co.), Fr. Paul Bull, "Missioners' Handbook" (Henry Froude).

2. **Mission Services in Church.**—Here, of course, there is room for infinite variety, and need of careful adaptation to local conditions.

In some parishes a simple mission service after Evensong on Sunday, or even at the usual hour of Sunday evening service (Evensong being said earlier), may be useful. The optical lantern is of great use, not merely as an " attraction," but as an invaluable means of teaching and of bringing home the reality of the gospel story. There is need of a careful choice of slides (the Church Army have a large supply), and obviously of a trustworthy operator.

3. **Mission Services in Public Halls or Theatres.** —In many places there is a considerable number of people who will not commit themselves by coming to church, but who will attend a mission service in a theatre or a public hall. It is surely well that we should try to reach them. If such services can be held regularly (say at 8 P.M.) throughout the winter, the clergy or their workers will have opportunity of coming into personal touch with constant attenders, and solid results may follow. Even where such services are only held at rare intervals, *e.g.*, on Good Friday evening, real good may be done.

4. **Preaching in the Open Air.**—It is sometimes said that open-air preaching is "played out." It is true that in some places the open-air meeting is so common and familiar that the very people whom it is intended to help keep out of its way. Nevertheless there is still a real opportunity for the Church to come out into the open. The character of the service will be determined by the nature of the locality, *e.g.*, one parish may contain (*a*) some stand in an important centre of a town where a large congregation may be gathered if their attention is arrested ; (*b*) side streets or courts where there will be no large gathering round the preacher, but a considerable audience at doors and windows.

In every case there is need for great care in preparation ; a company of faithful men and women should always go with the preacher to form a nucleus of the congregation and to help in the singing ; the hymns should be well chosen ; sometimes (as at the Woolwich Crusade) a really good solo has proved effective ; the preacher should be forcible and thoroughly human, carefully avoiding a "pulpit voice" and conventional language.

Sometimes it is good to march out in procession with clergy and choir in robes ; sometimes the plainest and simplest methods should be followed; there is no universal rule.

Intercessions in the open air—especially in the neighbourhood of a war-shrine—may be most reverent and real. The people will readily take part in the response if the prayers are in Litany form.

Rogation-tide processions are too well known and understood to need any special description.

Lay speakers (men and women) may give great assistance, only every address should be short.

The Church Army has great experience in open-air work, and many useful suggestions will be found in their publications.

5. **In Special Places, by Invitation.** — (*a*) *In Homes.*—At the time of the National Mission Message and afterwards many parish priests arranged for meetings in private houses, not by any means always the houses of "the poor." Obviously such meetings can only be by invitation. Probably such meetings should be intermittent rather than held in regular succession : they offer great possibilities for good.

(*b*) *In Lodging Houses.*—Here also there is need of great courtesy and consideration.

(*c*) *Factories and Workshops.*—Short dinner hour services are an established institution in many factories. The invitation of the employers can generally be secured. It is even more important to secure the sympathy and goodwill of the *works committees*, which happily are becoming a regular institution. After all, we have no business to intrude ourselves in the hard-earned dinner hour of the workers against their will. Where the clergy are already in sympathetic touch with the working people they will secure a glad hearing for their message.

Brevity and punctuality are obviously indispensable.

6. **Pilgrimages of Prayer.**—These have proved to be of great value in country parishes.

The pilgrims aim at delivering a simple and direct message. They are sent by the Bishop's commission. They stay in various houses, and visit all the homes, rich and poor alike, showing that the mission is not only to "the poor." They always make it clear that the visit is of distinct spiritual purpose. They hold mission services in churches or schoolrooms or in the open air.

7. **Crusades.**—Special efforts made by a large band of workers, clergy, laymen, and women, in some great industrial centre.

"Their chief characteristic is that they are of a simple and informal nature, the church evangelists mixing freely with the industrial workers, endeavouring to establish a means of appeal. Care should be taken that a sustained effort of consolidation should immediately follow the crusade."

CHAPTER VI

PREACHERS AND TEACHERS

AMONG those men who, possessing gifts of the Spirit,
are themselves our Lord's gifts to His Church, St.
Paul seems to distinguish between prophets, evangelists, and pastors and teachers.[1] It is beside the
mark to attempt exact distinctions between these
three ministries of the Word. The prophet is a
preacher who has a special insight into the divine
purpose, and a power of bringing it home to men's
hearts: with God's inspiration he speaks for God.
The evangelist is a preacher whose special mission
is that of leading men by conversion into living
touch with Christ. Conversion is one of the aims,
perhaps the chief aim, of all preaching ; but, as conversion is only the beginning of Christian life and
conduct, the minister of God's word seeks also to
deepen and strengthen the moral and spiritual life
of his hearers.

Again, it is not possible to draw a hard and fast
line between the preacher—whether he be prophet
or evangelist or the possessor of humbler gifts—and
the teacher of the flock. No doubt it will be said
that the preacher reaches the conscience through the
emotions, the teacher through the intellect. But, as
the soul of man is not made in water-tight com-
partments, a preaching which is purely emotional
will be vapid, and a teaching which is severely in-

[1] Eph. iv. 11 ; *cf.* 1 Cor. xii. 28, 29.

tellectual will be arid. Any preacher who is worth his salt will try to set forth the truth, and every teacher who believes the Christian creed to contain " words of eternal life " will appeal to the motives which may translate belief into action.

I. The Qualities of the Preacher and Teacher.— At all events there are certain conditions which must be fulfilled in the ministry of the word, of whatever kind it may be.

(1) We must have a message to give and must speak with conviction. The truth of the Christian revelation certainly does not depend on our apprehension of it. But the influence of our preaching does depend on the conviction with which we have laid hold on the truth, or rather on the power with which the truth has laid hold on us. A good preacher is not indeed always talking about his own experiences, but he knows Whom he has believed, and the message goes home because it is real. Of course I do not mean that we are justified in dwelling only on those doctrines which make the most vital appeal to ourselves : along that road lies the danger of a mutilated Gospel. Our effort rather will be to make the whole Gospel our own by the closeness of our personal contact with Him who is the Truth.

(2) As there must be progress in our living experience of the truth, so there must be progress in our intellectual apprehension of it. More mischief is done by those who affect to despise intellect even than by those who attach an exclusive importance to it. We must be diligent students all our lives through. Some of us have listened to discourses which were dull and heavy because the preacher did not know how to unload the unwieldy masses of his learning. But for every sermon which owes its dulness to such a cause, there are hundreds which are uninteresting simply because the preacher does not know his subject. He is making his flock to drink

of stagnant waters, instead of from streams which are kept fresh by study, and thought, and prayer. Surely it is inexcusable that, with such a subject as is entrusted to us, we should ever be dull and uninteresting.

It is, moreover, the gravest fallacy to imagine that an ignorant man is likely to be " simple " in his teaching. Some of the simplest teaching which I have ever heard was given in Bishop Westcott's confirmation addresses: the simplicity was the outcome of the most profound learning.

(3) Another source of simplicity and of other qualities which make for effective preaching and teaching is large-hearted human sympathy. Bishop King, of Lincoln, used to say that teaching is like a game of dominoes : you have to be sure that your number corresponds with that of the other player : six is a good solid number, but it is useless if the other man has produced a two. We need knowledge not only of our own subject, but of the minds of those to whom it is presented. No doubt a study of psychology is useful : we can gain help from such writers as James or Starbuck. But while it is good to know about human nature in the abstract, it is better to know the living actuality. Therefore a priest who never gets among his people—the man who is too lazy or too shy to visit—can never strike home when he preaches. He will be ignorant of their language ; their modes of thought will be a closed book to him ; he will be blind to their virtues, and be living in a fool's paradise with regard to their sins. He will be as one who beateth the air. But if he goes in and out amongst them and enters into their interests with intelligent sympathy, and if he is known as a friend who shares their joys and sorrows, his teaching will touch their minds, and his appeal will come home to their hearts.

(4) It goes without saying that there must be care

in preparation. "Some men prepare their sermons and some men prepare themselves." The latter business is doubtless more important, but each sermon needs painful thinking and working out. We will not discuss the respective merits of read sermons or of those delivered without manuscript. The question depends on a man's gifts, but I believe that there are few who cannot learn by hard practice to be independent of their script, and there are occasions (*e.g.*, open-air preaching) when a read sermon is impossible. There is much truth in Bacon's saying, "Reading makes a full man, writing makes an exact man, speaking makes a ready man." Most of us can acquire the "readiness," but a preacher (and still more a teacher) must be an "exact" man, and therefore he will do well, for many years after his ordination, to make a practice of writing his sermons, whether or no he uses the manuscript in preaching.

It is impossible to deal fully with the planning and working out of a sermon or instruction. No two men can follow exactly the same method. One subject, one sermon, is a good general rule, and the choice of that subject will be a simpler problem if the preacher adopts the plan of continuous teaching, about which more will be said presently. The preacher will read and make notes on such authorities as he has at hand. Of course he will seek God's guidance; then he will plan out a sketch of his discourse, making his points clear, considering his illustrations, but taking care that his teaching shall not be buried under them. Then he will get to work on the sermon, trying to make the introduction arresting but not over-long, and determining above all that he shall bring home to his hearers some one clear point of faith and practice.

There is one real difficulty which must be faced. The number of sermons and addresses which many parish priests are expected to produce is simply appalling. Many of the younger clergy are not their own masters in this matter, and they find it quite impossible carefully to think out and write out all their addresses. As time goes on, if they continue to be students, it will become less difficult for them to speak, with little preparation, out of the fulness of heart and mind. In the beginning of their priesthood [1] they may with a quite clear conscience, provided they work out (say) one sermon a week, borrow from the armoury of the tried warriors ; only they will acknowledge their debt, and, unless they are Davids, will not be too ready to wield the sword of the giant!

One apparently small matter is of first-rate importance. The most excellent sermon is useless if it is inaudible, and loses its power if it is badly delivered. Most men need to learn the art of voice production, and we are unfortunate indeed if we cannot find some kindly critics who will save us from mannerisms and from the abomination of the " pulpit voice." One of the best speakers of my acquaintance is ineffective because he delivers his words at such a break-neck pace that it is impossible to follow him, and most of us have " sat under " preachers who have ruined excellent matter by drawling or mumbling, or by dropping their voice at the critical point of their sentences.

(5) There is some relief in turning from these details to that which is central. The vital condition of good preaching and teaching is prayer and meditation. The supreme need of the teacher is that he should care for what he teaches. If we are intensely interested in a subject, absolutely on fire about it, our hearers will catch the flame. That is true in all educational work, but it is doubly true of the great subject of all. The subject of our teaching is JESUS CHRIST—who He is, what He stands for, what He

---

[1] In most dioceses strict limits are set on the amount of preaching to be imposed on deacons.

calls on us to do, what He does for us. It is only by prayer, by thinking about Him, by dwelling near Him, that we can be kindled with the fire of His Spirit. No priest who, seeking the guidance of the Holy Spirit, spends half an hour daily in meditation, will ever wholly fail as a pastor and teacher.

II. **The Need of Teaching.**—As we are called on to preach as well as to teach, it seemed best to speak first of the qualities which are needed for both duties alike. There will always be a place for preaching, but it is generally felt that the supreme need of the day is clear and capable teaching. The urgency of the need is evident on all sides. As the chaplains to the forces all rejoice together over the fine quality of the men, so with one consent they deplore the prevailing ignorance of the Christian faith. Many of us could have foretold their verdict. Our failure to teach more than a very few has been manifest for long enough.

If there is one region in society which Christian teachers have most lamentably neglected it is the "educated class." No doubt there are some whose education is a cloak for priggishness—

> "There's a new tribunal now,
> Higher than God's, the educated man."

But there is a large body of really educated men and women, among whom members of the working class are more and more taking a place, for whom we have done nothing. Much that has been written about "public school religion" is quite out of date. In some of the best public schools for boys and high schools for girls the religious teaching is good, though there is a large number of secondary schools for which so much cannot be said. But what adequate attempt have we made to present the faith to those who have left school and crave for some sympathetic teacher who will help them to see the reasonableness and beauty of Christian truth? It is easy to meet with evidence of the ignorance of that truth among cultivated people. It is pathetic, for example, to find a popular modern writer who combines with a grotesque caricature of Christian doctrine a real insight into truths which, whether he likes it or not, are essentially Christian.

It is perhaps worth while to summarise some of the commonest misapprehensions which only patient teaching can correct.

(1) There are false ideas about God. He is represented either as a far-off supreme Being, a sort of motor at the back of beyond; or as an arbitrary tyrant ("why does not God stop the war?"); or as an easy-going Governor of the universe, who does not mind what his creatures do; anything except the God of infinite splendour, holiness, and love, who is revealed in Jesus Christ, the Father who calls for the willing response of His children to His own infinite love.

(2) The whole *rationale* of our religion is misunderstood. It is supposed to be a self-regarding, self-saving concern, instead of a religion of life and power, an inspiration for fellowship and self-sacrificing service.

(3) We still suffer from the crudest conceptions of the verbal inspiration of the Bible. As the "Student in Arms" puts it, the average soldier thinks that to be a Christian means "believing that the whale swallowed Jonah and that you must not amuse yourself on a Sunday." We want to make it clear that our belief in the inspiration of the Bible does not imply the historical accuracy of every detail, and that we welcome scholarly and scientific investigation (sometimes called "criticism"), provided that it is not based on questionable quasi-philosophic assumptions. While we must help people to value the Old Testament, with its record of the revelation

which God made " in many parts and many fashions "
to prepare them for the perfect revelation when
" He spake to us through His Son," we must guard
against the supposition, by no means obsolete even
now, that the moral teaching given anywhere in
the Bible is equally true and valuable.

(4) There is much misconception about the moral
teaching of our religion. It is supposed to consist
mainly of a series of prohibitions, and to lay little
stress on the robust and heroic virtues. We need,
we will not say, less of the ten commandments, but
certainly a great deal more of the two great Gospel
principles, " Thou shalt love the Lord thy God,"
" Thou shalt love thy neighbour," with all that they
imply of courage and self-sacrifice.

But the need for clear and efficient teaching does
not arise only from the duty of dispelling error. It
is the duty of *Ecclesia docens* to interpret the
Christian faith to the men of each generation, " in
terms of current thought and aspiration."[1] No doubt
the invitation to "restate the Creed" sometimes
comes from those who want us to discard the old
Creed and concoct a new one of our own. But the
truth entrusted to us is not ours that we should play
fast and loose with it : if the facts enshrined in the
Creed were ever true, they are true for all time. We
may, however, rightly and reasonably be asked so
to express and explain the Christian faith that men
may see how completely it meets our modern needs.
Modern thought is not necessarily true because it
is modern, and the "spirit of the age" is by no
means altogether good ; but we must be ready to
welcome new light wherever we find it, and to bring
out of our treasures things new and old. We must
at least understand what men are thinking. The
good teacher is ready to stimulate inquiry rather
than to repress it, and his one desire must be that

[1] See " N.M. Report on Teaching," p. 18.

teacher and taught together shall seek the guidance of the Holy Spirit, who leads us into all truth.

III. **Some Principles of Teaching.**—(1) If we are to drive away error and meet the needs of current thought, the first necessity is for *positive and constructive teaching*, as opposed to mere negations. I have said that we must make it clear that we welcome "criticism." But the Archbishop of York is right when he says "it is not our business to argue vexed points of scholarship, or to obtrude the latest fancies of the critical imagination. We have simply to teach that positive revelation of which the Bible is a record, in language which brings no trace of the disputes of the schools. We have to teach men to know with a real human sympathy the lives, the history, the characters of the Bible writers . . . our ambition should be to restore their Bible to Englishmen, and to restore it enriched and quickened by a truer knowledge and a wiser faith."[1]

There is no sphere in which this positive teaching is more needed than in that of Christian morals. Let me add two examples to illustrate what I said about the positive Gospel law of love.

> (a) With regard to the supremely important subject of the Lord's Day, we shall do little or no good by laying down rules of what is not to be done. The question is what we are to do to make use of a good gift of God. Love to God calls us to worship Him; love to our neighbour requires that we should do all that we can to enable him to get his Sunday rest. If those principles are established, everything else will follow.

> (b) With regard to sexual morality, we may sometimes have to speak about the ugli-

[1] "Opportunity of the Church of England," p. 23.

ness of lust, and its awful results on body
and soul. But we shall do more good by
speaking positively of the sacredness of
the body, the beauty of real love between
man and maid, and the happiness of the
home to which that love should lead.

Positive teaching will also keep us from the futilities
of controversy. There are still men who devote so
much care to attacking the religion of other people
that they have little time for stablishing their own.
Whenever it is our duty to banish and drive away
any erroneous and strange doctrines, our best tactics
will be to put the positive truth in possession ; darkness will vanish in the presence of light. It is always
good to dwell on the great foundation truths which
unite us rather than on the beliefs (often quite
secondary) which divide us. If anyone fails to
understand me, let him read those two excellent
books, "The Religion of the Church" and "The
Creed of a Churchman"; they come from what we
should commonly suppose to be quite different
schools of thought, but because they are positive
and constructive, they show a wonderful agreement
at almost every point.

(2) The positive truth of the Christian faith is a
truth which can be *taught with authority*. And as
we have our Lord's message to deliver, we ought like
Him to speak as men having authority and not as the
scribes. Only, in the first place, let us be quite sure
that it is His message which we give ; and secondly,
let us not lay claim to an authority which our hearers
do not recognise. If we are speaking to convinced
Church people who want to know the authoritative
teaching of the Church, it is reasonable, if we really
know our subject, to say "the Church teaches this
or that." But we ought also to help those who are
not convinced, who have some doubts (sometimes,

alas! justifiable) as to our knowledge of what the Church teaches, and who in any case are wholly unimpressed by our assumption of authority. It is hardly cynical to say that large parts of the British public are more ready to accept the authority of their favourite journalist or the latest popular novelist than that of the Church, as represented by its ministers.

Therefore, while it is an immense strength to ourselves to know that we have the authority of the Church behind us, we shall not be too ready to claim it. We shall try to commend our teaching to every man's conscience in the sight of God, and we shall often approach the conscience through the intelligence. The Church of Christ has never been obscurantist, never regarded the faith as something of which we have any cause to be intellectually ashamed.

> "I say the acknowledgment of God in Christ,
> Accepted by the reason, solves for thee
> All problems in this world and out of it."

We want to see this clearly for ourselves, and to help others to see it.

(3) It is on that great central truth, "God in Christ," that the whole body of Christian doctrine depends. And it is important that we should teach the Christian faith as a connected and articulate whole. It is too commonly regarded as a chapter of accidents. There is urgent need for continuous teaching on great subjects. Courses on the Creed, the Lord's Prayer, the Commandments in the light of the Sermon on the Mount, or on the Person and Character of our Lord, are of immense service. Some men, who have the power of expository teaching, can go through a book of the Bible Sunday by Sunday. Others can take some one great idea—*e.g.*, prayer, penitence, communion with God—and follow out our Lord's and the apostles' teaching on it. Other examples might easily be given. The point is that a connected

plan is better than a casual congeries of random subjects.

While we want to dwell on the central truths, yet there is need of a full gospel. Some of the new religions, such as "Christian Science" and "Spiritualism," would never have existed if the Church had preached the whole faith; their strength lies in the element of truth which their weird errors contain, or even conceal. A full and courageous teaching of the supremacy of spirit over matter and of the communion of saints is the most effective way of meeting what we cannot but hold to be falsity and misbelief.

Here, then, is our task—to teach the whole truth as it is in Jesus, to proclaim it as men having authority, and yet to commend it to the minds, and hearts, and consciences of our hearers; to keep nothing back, but to maintain the proportion of faith. We could not dare to take such a work upon ourselves. We can only fall back on the certainty of our call and our commission, and claim our Lord's promise, "the Comforter shall guide you into all truth."

APPENDIX TO CHAPTER VI

IT may be useful to mention some special methods for the teaching of adults.

1. **Instructions in Church.**—In many places it might be possible to separate the "preaching and teaching" from the ordinary offices of the Church. The only sermon which the Prayer Book directs is at the Eucharist. At that service and at Matins and Evensong there might be a very short discourse, and a fuller instruction, with a few prayers and hymns, given at another time. Special addresses to special classes of hearers are of course a common feature of many parishes. It is very much to the good when in large centres of population different parishes combine for the purpose of providing really first-rate courses of instruction in some convenient church.

2. **Lectures.**—In many towns, lectures on important points of Christian faith and practice, or on the Bible or Church history, are given in some central hall. This again is a case for inter-parochial action. Questions and discussion may be encouraged. Lectures on Christian Evidence are sometimes very useful. It is more than usually necessary to secure a first-rate man for them.[1]

3. **Bible Classes.**—These vary from the immense Bible class of a Lancashire town, with perhaps 1,000 men on the books, to the small group, and the methods must of necessity differ according to circumstance. Where the class is very large the members

---

[1] Help may be obtained from the Christian Evidence Society.

can take little part except perhaps by reading some of the verses in the selected portion all together. In a smaller class it is all to the good for the members to take the fullest possible share in the work of study.

4. **Study Circles.**—The essence of a study circle is that it should be small in numbers, and that every member of it should contribute to the common task. One is chosen as leader, and at each session some subject is assigned to some one member for special elucidation. The subjects may be very various— some part of the Bible, a period of Church history, some aspect of missionary work, social questions, etc.

5. **Tutorial Classes.**—The methods which have been found useful in the Workers' Educational Association have been applied with great success to the study of theology. The essence of the method is complete liberty for the students with regard to choice of subject and of tutor.

6. Methods for the promotion of study among the clergy themselves will be referred to in Chapter XIV.

CHAPTER VII

MINISTRY OF THE SACRAMENTS—
BAPTISM AND CONFIRMATION

"GRACE and Truth came by Jesus Christ." So far we have thought of the Ministry of the Word of Truth. Now we turn to the Ministry of Grace, by which we understand the very life and power of God Himself, freely given to us in our Lord Jesus Christ through the outpouring of His Spirit.

I. **Sacramental Grace.**—This is not a treatise on theology. It is not my purpose to deal fully with the subject of sacramental grace, or to explain why we believe that God, who can and does bestow His grace freely in any way that He chooses, uses the sacraments as His special and regular means of uniting us to Himself. It is evident that we find everywhere the "outward and visible signs of inward and spiritual grace." The whole order of the world is sacramental. Visible nature, as God has made it, is everywhere a sign and symbol of spiritual truth—

> "Earth's crammed with heaven
> And every common bush ablaze with God."

When we turn from the world of nature to the life of grace we clearly recognise that all the Christian faith radiates from the truth—"the Word became flesh and dwelt among us." That Word is with us still, and His methods are still the same. "The gifts of God in Christ are not to depend upon our subjective feelings, but upon the will of God, and are guaranteed to our wills by the outward sign."

It will help us to a right ministration of the sacraments if we bear two principles in mind.

(1) While each child of God must be in direct personal relationship with Him, He does not treat us as isolated units. He brings us into His family, and the means whereby He leads us into and keeps us in fellowship with Himself are intended also to strengthen our fellowship one with another in His Church.

(2) We have bodies as well as souls; our bodies as well as our souls are capable of redemption; and it is congruous with all that we know of God's dealings with mankind that spiritual realities should be brought home to us through our bodily faculties.

We need not discuss the number of the sacraments, whether they are two, or seven, or many more. No one denies that there are two great sacraments which stand out above the rest: first, because we have the record in the Gospels of their institution by our Lord during His earthly ministry; and secondly, because they mark, in a unique manner, our incorporation into the Body of Christ, and the constant renewal of our fellowship with Him. But the Prayer Book does not forbid us to speak of other sacramental rites as sacraments. Some of those lesser sacraments will be spoken of in this book, but our attention will be fixed chiefly on Baptism and the Holy Communion.

II. **Holy Baptism.**—In the sacrament of Baptism our Lord receives us into living relationship with Himself, while at the same time He incorporates us into the Christian society. "As many of you as have been baptized into Christ have put on Christ":[1] "by one Spirit are we all baptized into one body."[2] Sacraments are real instruments of God's grace: but it must be a very bad theology which lends itself to the accusation of treating them as "magical charms." God begins the good work,

[1] Gal. iii. 27   [2] 1 Cor. xii. 13.

but it cannot take effect in a man's soul without his co-operation. The grace requires the faith, and the faith requires the grace, just as both violin and bow are necessary before music can be made. In early days this was evident enough. No man was admitted to holy Baptism until he had declared his purpose of fighting against the evil, of believing God's truth, and of trying to do God's will. When, at a very early period, it became the custom to baptize in infancy the children of believing parents, so that each stage of human life might be consecrated to God and receive His grace, the Church required security that such children should grow up to know Him whose members they had become, and be trained to take a living and working part in the Christian family. The appointment of sponsors was devised for this end : they represent the Church, and are intended to afford some guarantee that the child shall grow up to be a Christian, responding by repentance and faith to God's great gift.

Thus there are two conditions—among others—which must be fulfilled if baptism is rightly administered. (1) The recognition of membership in the society. (2) Security that the child shall be brought up as a Christian.

Now there can be no question that in the ordinary practice of most town parishes these two conditions are very inadequately fulfilled. A special time—on a week-day evening or a Sunday afternoon—is appointed, when no one will be present except those who accompany the child, and when it is doubtful whether the right number of sponsors will be present, and still more doubtful whether they will afford any security whatever for the Christian training of the child.

In a town parish, where baptisms are numerous, the difficulty is very great. I cannot pretend to offer a satisfactory solution. Let us first consider how

we may at least try to secure the Christian upbringing of the child. If convenient hours are chosen for
the service it will never be really impossible for
even the poorest family to find sponsors who can
attend. It is far more doubtful whether they will
be the right sort of people to look after the child's
spiritual interests. Probably two lines of action must
be taken. First, let all the parishes in a town deanery
agree to take common action, and to require that
at least three days' notice shall be given of every
baptism : if this is kindly done and the reasons for
it explained, parishioners will soon acquiesce. Then
before the baptism the family will be visited, and
the need of the right kind of sponsor will be shown :
it is generally accepted, that, in spite of the ancient
rule, the parents can stand. Secondly, some of the
regular communicants of the parish may be asked
to hold themselves in readiness to act as sponsors
for children whose parents would welcome their
aid. The plan is not easy, but it is not impossible,
and offers a really useful sphere of Christian work.

Doubtless in a "well-worked parish" other means
may be found for keeping watch over all children
who have been baptized, and commending them to
another parish if the family changes residence.[1] But in
big and under-staffed parishes this is really impossible,
though something may be done where the methods
of reformed Sunday school, with its family baptism
register, are adopted.

We turn to the other difficulty. How shall baptism
be so administered that the idea of admission to the
fellowship of the Christian Society shall be recognised ? It is certain that baptisms ought always to
be at a public service, when the congregation can
take their part in welcoming and praying for the new
member. In a small parish this is possible, but

[1] This is one of the many ways in which a good branch of the
Mother's Union can render aid.

where there is a large population we should find that there would hardly be a Sunday Evensong without a baptism, and most congregations would rebel. At all events we could arrange that at least at one Children's Service and one Sunday Evensong in each month there shall be public baptisms. The baptism should be conducted with solemn ceremonial, and on the " Baptism Sunday " Evensong could be shortened (surely no bishop would refuse permission), with a special psalm and one lesson; the choir would proceed to the font, and immediately after the baptism a short sermon could be preached, followed by the Nunc Dimittis and the rest of Evensong. People enjoy such a service and (what is more to the point) it is very good for them. One of the most impressive services in which I have ever taken part was an adult baptism at Evensong on an Easter Day.

A few words may be added about adult baptism and private baptism.

At almost every confirmation it will be found that some of the candidates have not been baptized, and at various times men and women will present themselves for baptism. In every case, of course, careful preparation is requisite, every whit as full as for confirmation, which will doubtless follow at the earliest opportunity. Difficulty sometimes arises in the case of young children who are no longer babies, but have hardly reached "years of discretion." Should sponsors be found for them, or should they answer for themselves? Probably the line might be drawn at the age of about twelve.

The parish priest will be ready at any moment to answer the call to baptize a sick child. The Prayer Book allows discretion as to the length of the service, but, unless circumstances render it impossible, the priest will wear surplice and stole, and will quietly and kindly help those who are present to take a reverent part in the service. If the sick child recovers, the priest will take care that he is received into the Church. He will also take occasion to explain from time to time to the congregation the ancient rule of the Church that in a case of emergency a lay member of the Church may baptize, pouring water on the child in the name of the Father, and the Son, and the Holy Ghost.

III. **Confirmation.**—Baptism finds its completion in Confirmation, when, through the laying on of the bishop's hands, special gifts of the Holy Spirit are bestowed. The candidate comes to "be confirmed," that is, to be strengthened by the power of God. It is unnecessary here to dwell on the teaching of the Bible, or the practice of the Church, with regard to this sacramental rite. Nor is it wise to attempt to define too exactly what is the operation of the Holy Spirit in confirmation, as compared with what He has already done in baptism. Perhaps it may be said that at baptism He enlists us in God's army, and that at confirmation He equips us with His armour and sends us forth to fight. He has been with us since our baptism ; at confirmation He enters our hearts with a special personal indwelling, and bestows on us those gifts which will enable us to exercise the priesthood which belongs to all members of the Church, for confirmation, like baptism, is a sacrament of fellowship in the divine society.

In the Church of England, confirmation (the strengthening by the Spirit) is associated with the renewal of the baptismal vows. It is untrue to say that the child "takes upon himself" at confirmation "the responsibility of his god-parents." He ought to have done that already. Whenever he says in the catechism, "Yes, verily, and by God's help so I will," he declares his responsibility for believing and doing what his sponsors promised for him. Nevertheless, the renewal of vows is a solemn and important thing : it represents that deliberate self-surrender, that dedication of the heart to God, which is our response to God's generous gifts, and the condition of their effective working in heart and will. The Church is more than justified in asking this evidence of earnest purpose before giving the effective sign of the Holy Spirit's grace.

(1) *The Right Age for Confirmation.*—The right age for confirmation is a vexed question. The Prayer Book requires that the child shall have reached "years of discretion," shall be "able to say the Creed, the Lord's Prayer, and the Ten Commandments," and shall be further instructed in the Church catechism. These directions are capable of different interpretations. A child may be able to repeat the Creed, etc., and even to say the Church catechism by rote at a very early age. On the other hand, instruction in the Church catechism presumably means more than a perfectly useless parrot repetition, and there are very few children who are capable of intelligent "instruction" in the more difficult parts of the catechism before (say) the age of twelve.

If we approach the question from the standpoint of Christian expediency, there is much force in the contention that a child is soon faced with great temptations, and needs all the grace he can find to enable him to "withstand in the evil day." Pushed to its logical extreme, this argument would lead us to the Eastern custom of infant confirmation. But there is at least good reason for giving the child his spiritual armour before the special difficulties of adolescence have to be faced; and, alas! in many homes troubles and temptations begin only too soon. On the other hand, if we think not merely of the individual, but of the society in which he is to become —with the help of his confirmation gifts—a working and fighting member, we shall take a stricter view of what "years of discretion" mean.

The fact is that there is no hard and fast rule.

The reasons given above seem to point to some such rule as that which most dioceses follow, namely, that twelve shall be the minimum age, with a loophole for exceptions in quite special cases. A wise parish priest will consider the circumstances of each candidate on their own merits, but he will not forget the claims of the Christian society as well as of the individual.

(2) *Preparation for Confirmation.*—The preparation of candidates for confirmation is one of the happiest bits of work in the life of a parish priest. It is brim full of opportunity. The purpose of it is to secure that the candidate shall come to his confirmation and his communion with an instructed understanding, a clear conscience, and a resolute will, in order that he may take his place as a full-grown member of the Christian family, ready to pray, to fight, to witness, and to work.

In gathering candidates together, the priest will soon find that whereas in some circles of society it requires courage to accept confirmation, in others it would need courage to refuse it. Parishes differ enormously in the readiness or reluctance with which candidates come forward. It is grievous if they lack this means of grace through sheer ignorance of what it means; it is far worse that a large number of candidates should be dragooned into confirmation, or should come to it merely because it is the proper and conventional thing to do. Therefore, in all cases it is desirable that at the very start the priest should say to possible candidates: "The preparation for confirmation is about to begin, and I cordially invite you to come; but you need not make up your mind about being confirmed till you have heard more about it: let there be a clear understanding that you and I are perfectly free—you to say to me that you had rather not be confirmed just yet, and I to say to you that you had better put it off for another year." No sort of reproach should be supposed to attach to candidates who are held back for a second year of preparation.

The Sunday school or catechism is the natural recruiting ground; where there is a Church day school, the teachers will be consulted, and the children of Church parents may be invited. But in every parish full opportunity should be given for older people to come forward. A priest who visits will find plenty of potential candidates. It is desirable to preach a sermon about sacramental grace in general and confirmation in particular, shortly before the time of preparation begins.

A priest cannot really " prepare " candidates. He can only help them to prepare themselves, or rather to place themselves under the guidance of the Holy Spirit. His part in the work is of three kinds: he can give class-instruction to groups of candidates; he can offer them spiritual help of a directly personal kind; and he can pray for them.

In the classes for teaching, much care will be needed in the grouping and classifying of candidates. Parts of the instruction may indeed be given to all the candidates together in the church. For other parts of it the formation of classes will be determined by sex, by age, and by knowledge.[1] The actual instruction must obviously depend on what the candidates already know. The first class will clearly deal with Confirmation itself—what it is, what it is not: what God will do for us, what He calls on us to do for Him. Then the course (varied in detail to suit the various needs) will follow the main lines

---

[1] A careful register of candidates is clearly necessary. It should include (*a*) name and address, (*b*) age, (*c*) day school? (*d*) Sunday school? (*e*) parents' consent? (*f*) where baptized? In any case where the baptism is doubtful, inquiry should be made of the church where the candidate thinks he was baptized. If there is still doubt, the candidate should be conditionally baptized.

of the Church catechism—what I am : what, as a Christian, I ought to believe : what, as a Christian, I ought to do : how I seek God's grace in prayer : how He gives us His grace in the sacraments. From first to last the candidate should clearly understand that confirmation is the door to Holy Communion : some of the actual instruction about that sacrament may sometimes be given in the interval between confirmation and first communion. They should also be clearly taught that the strength of the Holy Spirit is given them to enable them to be of use to God and their fellows.

In this work of instruction—which requires at least three months—the parish priest may well enlist the aid of under-shepherds. In many parishes there are laymen and women who are well qualified to help. For the plain, but careful and loving, instruction on the subject of sex, which can never safely be omitted, it is absolutely necessary that the girl candidates should come under the influence of some wise and pure-minded woman.

There are parishes where all the instruction is given to candidates individually. The paucity of staff generally makes this method impossible. But in every case it is of primary importance that the parish priest should see the candidates individually to offer them that personal spiritual help which cannot be given to a group or a class. If he is a man of sympathy, and has gained their confidence, the candidates will gladly come to him. Sometimes the ice may be broken by giving each candidate (after, say, the third instruction) some simple questions to answer in writing: one of the questions may be—" Do you wish to be confirmed ; if so, why ? " Times will then be arranged when each candidate can come and talk his answers over with the parish priest. By the second or third interview mutual confidence ought to be established, the candidate will be ready to speak of his special difficulties, help can be given to him in his prayers, and more good may be done than by many classes of instruction.

All candidates should clearly understand that it is open to them to make their confession to God in the priest's hearing, in order that they may receive the benefit of absolution according to the plan given us in the Prayer Book. In some cases such confession may rightly be recommended. But it is most unwise to press it, and it is absolutely wrong to make it a condition of confirmation. In the case of children, the parents' consent should always be obtained before they come to sacramental confession. The one essential thing is that all candidates should approach their confirmation with true repentance, that they should have made a real search into their own consciences, and confessed their sins to God, with a resolute purpose of amendment.

(3) In speaking of preparation for confirmation, I have been drawing on my own experience as a parish priest. With regard to the confirmation itself, my happy experience as a bishop in two dioceses has shown me with what reverent care, in almost every parish, the service is ordered, and how wonderful is the hope for these young lives under the guidance of the Comforter. But the experience of every bishop and every priest shows the necessity of constant pastoral care, if those who have been confirmed are to persevere as faithful communicants' as living and working soldiers and servants of Jesus Christ. Some possible methods of meeting thi need will be considered in the next chapter, but the priest will be giving his best help if he never ceases to present all and each before God in faithful intercession.

CHAPTER VIII

HOLY COMMUNION

THE subject of this chapter is central and vital. It is likely to be the shortest chapter in the book, partly because previous chapters have dealt with the Holy Eucharist, and still more because I prefer to leave the theology of so great a subject to writers whose learning and devotion are greater than my own.[1]

Every true priest gains in each succeeding year fresh experiences of the wonder, the awe, and the joy of this great sacrament. Our Lord is recognised by him in the breaking of bread. He does not care to argue as to the exact manner of our Lord's presence. He knows that Jesus, "who liveth and was dead," comes to be with us, to give to us the supreme gift,[2] Himself. As he celebrates the divine mysteries, he is vividly conscious that the true celebrant is the one High Priest, who leads us there into the heart of the mystery of divine redemption, and enables us to "plead and represent before the Father the sacrifice of the Cross."[3]

From this bare and meagre introduction to an inconceivably great subject, I pass to two matters which call for some practical consideration—our responsibility as celebrants, and the training of our communicants.

[1] I find myself in complete accord with Bishop Gore's " Body of Christ."
[2] Bishop Westcott's " Revelation of the Father," p. 41.
[3] " Archbishops' Reply to Pope Leo XIII.," Sect. xi.

I. **Our Responsibility as Celebrants.**—It is unnecessary to say that we have special need for care in our preparation. The office of celebrating this sacrament must never become "familiar" to us. Our reverence and our sense of unworthiness for so great an honour must be kept constantly fresh.[1] If we have the supreme privilege of a daily Eucharist (and readiness for that privilege is not to be found in every parish or in every priest) it is imperatively demanded of us that, by God's grace, we should retain a high spiritual level : frequency in celebrating or in communicating calls us to set apart more, not less, time for private prayer. Our peace must be kept fresh by penitence, our love by intercession, our joy by thanksgiving ; we must place ourselves in the hands of our High Priest that He may use us in this greatest of all ministries.

We are called to minister in the Church of England. The liturgy of that Church is not perfect ; but it unquestionably contains all that is essential. Some may wish for permission to adopt (*e.g.*) the liturgy of the 1549 Prayer Book as an alternative use ; in that desire they are entirely free from any sinister design, and they rightly feel that it is ungenerous to accuse them of disloyalty to the principles of our Church. But as long as the present order remains, we ought loyally to abide by it. It is right and reasonable that there should be various ceremonials in different churches, and I do not intend to give counsel on this subject. Certainly every priest, at his ordination, should seek advice and help from some trustworthy older brother as to the right way

[1] "If the simple lay communicant rarely ventures to draw near to Holy Communion without putting on the wedding garment of the guest of God, shall the celebrant penetrate deeper into the spiritual world and handle and consecrate the means of holiest grace without a preparation yet more thorough and complete ?"—Bishop Gott, " Parish Priest of Town," p. 179.

of celebrating, and it goes without saying that he ought not to accept a curacy in any parish where he cannot conscientiously conform, in all important matters, to the practice of his seniors. Whatever ceremonial is followed, a priest will try to be simple and natural, and unself-conscious when he celebrates : he will take care to be audible ; he will avoid peculiar gestures or intonations of his own invention, and fancies capriciously culled from continental usage. After all, there is a good English tradition which is wholly Catholic.

A word may be said about the communion of the sick. The Prayer Book clearly recommends and provides for celebration in the sick-room. It is possible, even in the poorest home, to celebrate the Holy Communion with perfect reverence. (I speak with experience of some of the worst slum parishes.) The priest will of course take with him all that is requisite, and it is possible in most cases to find some devout church worker who will help in the needful preparation. There is no question that many of our communicants greatly value the privilege of the complete service in their sick-rooms. But in parishes where there is a large number of communicants and a small staff of priests there is real difficulty in providing for sick communicants at the great festivals. Most bishops would grant permission in such cases to follow the primitive custom of conveying the Blessed Sacrament straight from the altar of the church to the sick person, and there is a strong case for allowing perpetual reservation, at certain convenient centres, and especially in hospitals, to provide for special emergencies.

Some of my brethren, who feel very strongly on this subject, will not accuse me of lack of sympathy if I add two words of counsel. First, the ancient Church principle of fasting communion is, I am convinced, right and sound. But the principle of

6

charity is superior to it: for example, chaplains at the front have sometimes been called on quite suddenly to celebrate Holy Communion for men who are unexpectedly summoned into action; in such cases they cannot doubt which way their duty lies. The same principle applies to cases where a priest who has broken his fast is suddenly called on to celebrate Holy Communion for a dying person. On such occasions strict rigorism is bad Christianity.

Secondly, this question of reservation is one in which the responsibility must rest with the chief pastor of a flock. There is really no question here of arrogating undue authority to the bishop. It is arguable—indeed it is sometimes strongly asserted—that under the present rule of the Church of England as laid down in the Prayer Book neither bishops nor anyone else can authorise reservation. But, as I said before, it seems reasonable to hold that the bishops have "lawful authority" to deal with special cases: if those who desire reservation do not recognise the authority of the bishops with regard to its permission and regulation, it is difficult to understand what authority the bishops are supposed to hold in any part or function of the Church's life.

II. **The Training of Communicants.**—I turn to one of the most important duties in our pastorate, the help which we offer our communicants in a right and reverent use of this sacrament, and in the life of prayer, of work and witness in the Christian family and the world outside, to which our Lord calls them, and for which He communicates His life and power to them. If we may reverently compare small things with great, just as our Lord trained the inner circle of His disciples that they might be light and salt and leaven to those around them, so we may set before ourselves the ideal of preparing our communicants to be a warm centre of Christian life and work in the whole parish. Of course this does not mean that they are to be prigs, always trying to "do good" to people or make edifying conversation. Our hope is that they will be simple, cheerful men and women, lads and girls, showing by their daily life what a natural and happy thing it is to follow Jesus. And let us not forget that many of them are likely enough to pass through fierce persecution in the factory or even in the home. Martyrdom is a real thing in many a town and village to-day.

For our younger communicants some shepherding is absolutely necessary. Indeed we are not justified in presenting children for confirmation unless we are prepared to keep in close touch with them afterwards. The best help can be given personally and individually. We are the under-shepherds of the Good Shepherd who knows His sheep by name. We shall deal with this later. But we want to have a family feeling among our communicants, and to give them the opportunity of strengthening one another. Therefore in most large parishes a Communicants' Guild or Union is really a necessity. Sometimes the men, the women, the lads, the girls each have a guild of their own. Experience shows that the lads at all events need to be dealt with separately, and it is best that they should be under the care of one member of the staff who is "good with lads." The Communicants' Guild should have a very simple rule, and should meet at intervals for prayer and instruction.

It is hardly necessary to say that the instruction need not always deal with the subject of the Holy Communion itself, though that sacrament touches our Christian faith at almost every point. We want our people to know who our Lord is, how we can pray in His name, how we can get back to Him when we have gone wrong, how we can live a life of fellowship with Him, how we can be of service to Him. We must know a good deal about our Lord Himself before we can gain much help from instructions as to His presence in the Blessed Sacrament. We are sometimes tempted to build the top storey before the foundation is laid.

Careful teaching about self-examination is certainly needed. Very few of the printed lists of self-examination questions seem to be adequate.[1] They are often far too negative, and they do not give nearly enough attention to those sins which our Lord most sternly condemned. St. Paul's great chapter on charity is a good mirror for convicting us of that selfishness which is at the root of all sin, and the twenty-third chapter of St. Matthew suggests searching questions for priest and people alike.

In our instruction of our communicants let us be on our guard against a selfish, merely individualistic idea of the Holy Communion. "We being many are one bread, one body, for we are all partakers of the one bread." But how many communicants look for a solitary place in church, consider and pray for their own needs alone, and never give a thought to their fellowship with those who kneel at the same altar, and with all the people of God, here and in Paradise. We thank God if their sense of personal fellowship with our Lord is real and strong; without it there is indeed no vital religion. But the Elder Brother can hardly be satisfied until there is a warm-hearted loving brotherhood among all who are one in Him.

[1] A very good one is to be found in the Bishop of Zanzibar's "Conquering and to Conquer," pp. 45-49.

CHAPTER IX

PERSONAL DEALING

THE Good Shepherd says—" I know My sheep, and My sheep know Me."[1] He knows His sheep by name. His under-shepherds must follow His example. The happiest and the most fruitful part of our work is to be found in the personal love and care of the individual members of our flock. The parish priest, whose relation to his people is that of a pope surrounded by his curia, or of a superior officer who may only be approached through an N.C.O., may be a good organiser, but will never be a good shepherd. Doubtless we must be content to do some of our work through committees and councils ; and committees are an excellent training-ground in wisdom and good temper, and in the happy art of getting things done, while we cheerfully allow others to obtain the credit for them. But no amount of committee work can ever take the place of a personal pastorate.

Here the country priest has a great advantage over his brother in a large town. In a small parish a priest can gain an intimate knowledge of every member of his flock. His position has its special difficulties and trials : while any pastor feels a personal sorrow when one of his spiritual children falls away, the parish priest of the town cannot afford to dwell on the disappointment ; he does his best for the wanderer,

[1] St. John x. 14.

but is obliged to turn to the many others who need his aid. The country priest has no such compensation : nevertheless it is easier for him to "know all his sheep by name," to intercede for them all, and to lead them all through his own personal touch into personal fellowship with the Good Shepherd.

I. **Opportunities.**—What opportunities has a parish priest for this personal relationship with his people? Any man of experience will feel the question to be superfluous. But it may be worth while to offer a few suggestions to those who are beginning their ministry.

The first answer is—visit, visit, visit ; of the opportunities which come to us in the homes of our people I shall speak in the next chapter. With our church officers, and choirs, and workers we have constant points of contact. In the Day school and Sunday school we can make friends with teachers and children. The occasions of a baptism, or marriage, or funeral give us the chance of personal sympathy and help at a time when they are specially valued. I have already spoken of the priceless opportunity afforded to us by confirmation. We can meet the men and the lads in the club ; sometimes we have a chance of visiting the factory, or workshop, or farm, and getting a friendly word with them there. There are the hundred and one occasions when people come to us for some kind of help or comfort, and when we have the chance of making friends with them. Best of all, one and another of our flock comes of his own accord for direct spiritual help ; how often they come depends on what sort of priests we are.

Indeed the number of our opportunities will vary in accordance with our characters and gifts. Even the natural gifts cannot be ignored. Some men have a genius for friendship ; the children will hang on to their coat-tails in the streets ; the lads will come round to their rooms ; the men will be glad of a crack with them; the hard-pressed working mother will almost welcome them on a washing day. What a splendid chance their gift of friendship gives them if only they will use it well. Their danger will be lack of thoroughness and dissipation of energy. Kindliness and good-will are a valuable raw material for spiritual influence. But it is more important that we should be of real spiritual help to a few, than that we should be on good terms with many. Friendship with ourselves should only be the means towards the end of friendship with God.

There are other men, with a true pastoral spirit, who are naturally shy, awkward, and inarticulate. They have no cause to be discouraged. The very effort exerted in overcoming their difficulty may increase the value of their work, and perhaps they are less liable to the danger of dissipated energy. After all, we cannot all be Dollings or Stantons. God knows what gifts we need, and we may be sure that they will not be withheld from those who wait on Him.

II. **Qualities Needed**.—What, then, are the gifts and qualities needed for the personal help and guidance of their flock?

(1) We must be filled with an earnest desire that our people should have that joy and peace which come from right relationship with God. This is what is meant by the old-fashioned phrase, "a love of souls"; it may be said that we do not love a man's "soul"—we love the whole man; but the pastor's love must be of the unselfish kind, which seeks to draw men not to himself, but to God, and it is the man's soul which seeks and finds God.

Where there is love there will be sympathy : and this is not merely pity felt at a distance, but a compassion which makes us one with our people in their joys and sorrows. St. Matthew reminds us that our blessed Lord's compassion cost Him much; after describing

His works of mercy he refers to the well-known prophecy, " Himself took our infirmities and bare our sicknesses." [1] We cannot "bear their troubles" as our Lord did, but we must learn from Him the power of a feeling heart, a seeing eye, and an outstretched hand : and these will cost us something. Moreover, our Lord's sympathy was perfectly and gloriously human : the Carpenter of Nazareth understood labour questions, and His parables show us how every side of human life, from the joy of the children playing in the street to the shrewdness of the business man, came within His ken. No one could say of Him : " He is very kind, but He does not understand my case." His perfect all-inclusive humanity is above and beyond us ; but we must at least try to understand and enter into the common interests of our people, and to learn that nothing which our Lord cared for can be really " secular." And we ought to take special pains to appreciate those whose good qualities and failings are least sympathetic to ourselves. This loving sympathy is a big thing. Doubtless it is a gift from God, but it is a gift which all may have and all may cultivate ; and the best way of increasing it is intercession.

(2) Nothing can take the place of love for our flock. But there are men who really care for their people and yet fail through lack of homelier qualities. A priest must be a gentleman. Of course that does not imply any class privilege : the clergy ought to be drawn from every class, and class should be the last thing they care for : there is no greater need in the Church to-day than that men of every station and degree who have not merely a desire for, but God's real call to, the ministry should be enabled to receive a full training for the priesthood. But whether their origin be with high or low, with rich or poor, they must be modest and kind-hearted, with the sense of honour which always plays the game, and the courtesy

[1] St. Matt. viii. 17.

which considers the feelings of others in small things
as well as great, and the unself-consciousness which
enables them to be at home without obtrusiveness in
every sort of society. In a word, they must be
gentlemen. The Lord Mayor of a certain city once
said, "As Lord Mayor I have neither politics nor
religion!" so a priest might say, with less equivocal
meaning, "As a priest I have neither class nor politics."

(3) We turn to a third quality akin to the last—
the natural reality and simplicity which come from
singleness of aim. Bishop Lightfoot used to say
that "the best diplomacy is the most transparent
simplicity." It is the virtue of those who are "wise
as serpents and harmless as doves." It is not
uncommonly joined with a keen sense of humour,
without which many of us would find it difficult to
get through a hard day's pastoral work. There is no
levity in being able to see the humorous side of
things: a good laugh will often save us from the folly
of "taking offence," and there are times when we
should be tempted to cry if we did not know how
to smile.

III. **All Things to all Men.**—Now let us see how
we may show our pastoral character in some of the
more difficult relationships which confront us. We
have a mission not only to "the faithful," but to all
the people in the parish who do not definitely refuse
our aid. We shall come across people of other
religions, we shall find very many who seem to be
indifferent and a few who are hostile, and occasionally
we shall encounter the positively evil. How are we
to deal with them?

(1) To Christians of other communions we shall
show frank and consistent good-will. If they are
convinced adherents of their own creed—whether it
be Roman Catholic or Protestant Nonconformist—
we shall not attempt to draw them away from it.
We really have quite enough to do in seeking the
conversion of the sinful and the careless. We shall

only try to help them to be faithful members of their own communion. They will often tell us that "we are all making for the one place," which no doubt is true enough : it is better for us to avoid the obvious rejoinder that one road may be much more direct and wholesome than another ; possibly we may suggest that "trying to get to a place " is not the highest way of looking at the Christian religion, and that we ought rather to think of "serving the One Master," and of trying to learn His will and to do it. We shall not pretend that we think alike, or that our differences are unimportant, but we shall recognise goodness as a fruit of the Spirit wherever we find it, and in many parishes we have cause to thank God that the Nonconformists or the Roman Catholics have kept the torch of Christian faith alight amid prevailing darkness. We shall think later on of various ways in which we can cordially co-operate with other Christians.

(2) We turn to those who seem to have very little Christianity at all. They are largely represented in all towns and most villages, and we are inclined to label them as "indifferent." This label, like many others, is misleading. They are often inarticulate Christians : there is a vague and diffused Christianity among them, the result of centuries of Christian tradition, which we have no business to despise : their ignorance is due to many causes, among which the uglier part of our industrial system is not the least important. Our right principle in dealing with them is to respect them, to avoid the fallacy of lumping them together in one class (why will people persist in talking about the Church "reaching the masses"?) and to show infinite patience in understanding the position and need of each. Let us, above all, avoid the mistake of letting them think that we are shopmen touting for their custom. Of course we let them see that they will be welcome at church : but our business is to lead them to a better knowledge of God first,

and then the desire for worship will follow. We shall show them that the church is not an emporium at which each can get his own spiritual wares, but the family of those who are out to serve God and their fellows. "Will you not come and help us?" is a more effective question than "Will you not let us help you?"

(3) There are many who seem indifferent. There are few who are hostile. Now and then we meet with one who calls himself an atheist. We shall not often do much good by argument. Even if we are well-equipped for that business, we shall find that the man has not the will to be convinced. If indeed he wants to believe the Christian faith we shall mostly find that he is the victim of ignorance, and perplexed with some difficulty about the verbal inspiration of the Bible, or some crude notion of the atonement; such men are seldom altogether hostile, and are well worth helping.[1]

There are others who frankly dislike the "parson," and who let us know it. Good temper and a sense of humour will often disarm them. A man who first greeted me by saying, "Your Christianity and mine are as much like one another as chalk and cheese," eventually became one of my firmest friends. His chalk was the social teaching of Christianity—minus its redemptive power; I tried to show him that he knew very little about my cheese. I hope he learnt something from me; I certainly learnt a good deal from him.

(4) Occasionally we come up against the thoroughly evil. I do not mean the sheep who have "erred and strayed" (sometimes into very foul pastures), and whom we try to bring home along the way of penitence, but the wolves, the Ahabs and the Herods, who need quite different treatment. What is our duty with regard to them? Something depends on

[1] Useful help in meeting unbelief may be gained from the Christian Evidence Society.

the answer to the question, "Do they in any way recognise our authority?" Elijah and St. John the Baptist boldly rebuked vice, but, after all, Ahab and Herod Antipas did in some measure recognise their right to speak. If the offender is nominally a "Churchman," there is some priest whose duty it is to deal with him. We shall not denounce the man; denunciation seldom avails anything. We shall certainly not write him letters of rebuke,[1] we shall do our best to see him, to win him to a better mind, if possible, but at least to remind him that there is a righteous Judge before whom we stand.

There are cases of brutal lust, of gross injustice or cruelty, or oppression of the poor, when it may be the duty of a priest to interpose with word, sometimes with deed, on behalf of the weak who are suffering wrong. In such cases it does not matter whether our authority is recognised or not. Any decent man would do what he could to break the power of a human wild beast. Possibly we shall win commendation for our courage: more probably we shall meet with abuse. We shall be in good company if we have patiently to "suffer for the truth's sake." Only in all cases where we attack wrongdoing we must be careful to be absolutely sure of our facts, and not take up the position that we believe an accusation to be true until it is proved to be false.

IV. **The Physician of Souls.**—We return from the wolves to the sheep, and to a consideration of a very important part of our personal work—how we can bring home along the road of penitence those who have lost themselves. To use a different metaphor, we are physicians of souls, and our work is to diagnose the moral and spiritual disease, to prescribe

---

[1] It may be worth while to say a word of warning as to the danger of writing "stiff letters." If we have a disagreeable thing to say, let us *say* it, never write it. An angry letter is almost always a rude letter, and a letter of rebuke will certainly be misunderstood.

the remedy, and to keep the soul under the care of the good Physician Himself.

There is one problem which is always difficult to solve. How can we combine uncompromising loyalty to the Christian standard with compassion for the sinner? It is those who are nearest to our Lord who can best find the answer. We are bound to remember that His strongest condemnation is of such sins as covetousness (as in the case of the Temple-traders), or of hardness of heart, pride, and self-complacency: with sins of human passion, such as those of the woman taken in adultery, or the woman in the house of Simon the Pharisee, He deals very mercifully, though He in no way palliates the sin. He taught us that "every one that looketh at a woman to lust after her hath committed adultery with her already in his heart." [1] Now we have to face the trouble that in many places the standard with regard to some sins, notably sins of sexual passion, is miserably low: we dare not make any compromise about it. Yet an attitude of rigorism [2] is likely to defeat its own ends; we shall always be ready to welcome even the first poor beginnings of repentance; and we shall never be harsh in our judgments. Moreover, public opinion will be more ready to accept our verdict on sins of passion, if it is evident that we are equally stern in our condemnation of greed, and injustice, and hardness of heart. For all alike, priest and people, and in all sins alike, the way of God's forgiveness (which brings with it

[1] St. Matt. v. 28.
[2] Some priests refuse marriage in church in cases where there is clear evidence of sin before marriage. They can hardly have thought out all that their action implies. It is more than probable that they will marry, with full honours, some who have been guilty of even worse sin than that of anticipating marriage, while they reject those whose sin has been by no means so grievous. There are right ways of upholding the Christian standard of purity; this is surely a wrong way.

cleansing, liberty, and restoration to moral health) must be the way of repentance. There is no need to spend time on familiar ground, and to dwell on the meaning of contrition, confession, and amendment. We ought to know from personal experience what is that spiritual sorrow for sin which is the result, not of morbid introspection, but of the vision of God's holiness and love,[1] how after honest examination of our consciences we ought to confess our sins to God, and in what direction the duty of restitution and amendment ought to lead us.

There is one remedy which we are bound to place freely within the reach of all our people. At our ordination this commission was given to us, "Whose sins thou dost forgive they are forgiven, and whose sins thou dost retain they are retained." The words refer to the charge given by our Lord to His whole Church on the first Easter day, and His commission is exercised by the priest as organ of the whole society : "He hath given power and commandment to His ministers to declare and pronounce to His people, being penitent, the absolution and remission of their sins."

I do not propose to deal with the history of sacramental confession and absolution, nor to argue at length the meaning of the Prayer Book directions given in the office for the visitation of the sick, and at the end of the first exhortation in the communion office. It seems perfectly clear that this means of grace must be open to all; it is, I believe, equally clear that the Church of England refuses to accept the comparatively late doctrine that there can be no assured forgiveness for sin (at least "mortal sin") except by way of the sacrament of penance.[2] My purpose is to deal with our practical duty in the matter. This is a way of healing committed to us ;

[1] Isaiah vi.

[2] See "Fulham Conference on Confession" (Dr. Moberly), pp. 34, 35, 36.

all have liberty to use it. We have no business to dragoon people into it; we have no right whatever to refuse it to those who earnestly desire it; the only case which ever came within my personal knowledge of a member of our own Church joining the Church of Rome was that of a woman who asked one of our priests to hear her confession, and met with a peremptory refusal; could one blame her for going where she could get the help which she wanted? All have liberty to use sacramental confession, to some we strongly recommend it, on none may we enforce it, though indeed in the case of notorious sin we must require some real assurance of repentance before the offender can be admitted to his communion.[1]

Let us remember that every faithful minister of religion, whatever communion he belongs to, is sure to " hear confessions "; the differentia of the ministry entrusted to us is that we are called on to give absolution; we believe that " our Lord has given authority to His Church to absolve all sinners who truly repent and believe in Him," and " by His authority committed to us " we absolve them from their sins in the Name of the Blessed Trinity.

A young priest ought not to exercise this ministry, save under exceptional conditions, for some time after his ordination, and he will doubtless seek advice from some experienced older brother. He will certainly be better able to do this work if he makes use of sacramental confession for the good of his own soul. A few words of counsel may be given here.

(1) It is needless to say that knowledge gained in confession must be absolutely sacred. Neither directly nor indirectly may it be divulged.

(2) Confessions should be heard in church. It is often desirable that a third person should be present in the church.

[1] Questions of excommunication should be referred to the bishop.

(3) In the examination of conscience which precedes confession, help may often be given by some godly layman or woman. The priest should not ask questions of the penitent unless there is real reason to think that some sin is being kept back, or for the explanation of something which is ambiguous.

(4) Almost all those who (under our present conditions) seek this help, are in need of heartening and encouragement. They really desire to conquer their sins, and we want to assure them of the reality of God's cleansing and strengthening grace.

(5) Our business is not primarily to offer counsel and direction, but to give the assurance of God's forgiveness. The counsel that we give must aim at the enlightening and enabling of the individual soul. We are out to strengthen men's consciences, not to make them dependent on our " direction." At the same time we ought to be diligent students of moral theology, in order that we may deal with difficult questions of conscience. There is no part of our work which calls so loudly for earnest study, for ever-deepening spiritual experience, and for obedience to the guidance of the Holy Spirit.

Finally, in this and all our work as physicians of souls, let us remember that penitence is a gift of God, which grows to perfection just in so far as we are sure of God's forgiveness. He is no tyrant before whom we grovel. He is the Father who meets His children more than half way : we humble ourselves before Him that He may lift us up and enable us to stand on our feet. In penitence we find spiritual health, and the measure of our contrition is the measure of our peace and joy. With that peace in our hearts we go out to make war ; and in the security of that joy we are prepared to serve Him wherever He may choose to call us.

CHAPTER X

THE HOME

OUR aim is that our people may have life, and have it
abundantly. Our ministry of the word and sacraments, and all our pastoral work, seek to lead our
people into union with God in Christ, and into fellowship with one another, in order that they may follow
Christ in His life of love, and offer that service to
which He has called them. If there is one sphere in
which that life may be pre-eminently fulfilled and
that service rendered, it is the home. Our Lord
loved the home : the thirty years of preparation for
His ministry were spent in the home at Nazareth :
His first sign was wrought at the founding of a home :
He blessed the mothers and the children. St. Paul
was wholly true to His teaching when he said that
from the divine Fatherhood "every family (fatherhood) in heaven and earth is named." [1]

A Christian home is the "masterpiece of applied
Christianity." Thank God there are many homes in
England, representing all classes in society, where
the good leaven has been at work. Here the husband
and wife are joined in perfect love and loyalty, rejoicing in a growing comradeship and mutual sympathy, while they never cease to be "in love with"
one another ; here parents and children are united in
close affection, with an authority, on the one side,
which has nothing of the despot about it, and, on the

[1] Eph. iii. 15.

7

other side, a respect which ripens into the warmest friendship : here brothers and sisters enjoy that frank candour, that happy give and take, that unselfish care for one another's interests, which make strife unthinkable. Here there is a common loyalty and devotion which no separation can mar, and which death itself cannot destroy. These are the families where Christ loves to dwell, and they could not indeed be so marked with His likeness unless He dwelt among them. These are the homes where the parents have taught their children how to pray, and in which it is natural and inevitable that parents and children should kneel together to offer their united prayer and praise to the Father of all.[1] Few families, it may be said, attain to this ideal. And we confess, with all possible sympathy, that the stress of modern life and the outward conditions under which many families are compelled to live are ruinously destructive of home life. How can a man be a father to his children when he goes to work before they get up, and returns after they are in bed? What prospect is there of physical or moral health when the whole family is huddled together in two or three rooms, without a chance of privacy or even of decency? The marvel is that God works such miracles of grace among those whose environment is altogether against them. Nevertheless we are "tempting God" if we complacently allow such conditions to continue. It is difficult to be tolerant of those who think it "unspiritual" to be interested in housing questions.[2]

Meanwhile we must do the best we can, and while it is our duty to uphold the principles on which the

[1] In some dioceses a strong effort was made at the time of the National Mission Message to encourage family prayer, and much good was the result. A parish priest should always be ready to offer to come and help the parents in making a beginning. It is well also to provide simple forms of prayer.

[2] See Chapter XIII., pp. 144, 147.

life of the family is based, it is the privilege of the
parish priest to be welcomed in many homes, to be
the trusted friend of the parents, the big brother of the
children, and to share the joys and sorrows of all alike.

I. **Marriage.**—The home is built on marriage.
Every faithful priest will uphold the Christian ideal
of marriage. Our Lord's standard is quite clear,
"Whosoever shall put away his wife saving for the
cause of fornication" (the exception does not appear
in the parallel passage in St. Mark) "causeth her to
commit adultery: and whosoever shall marry her
that is divorced committeth adultery." [1]

This is not the place to deal at length with the
question of divorce.[2] We must be perfectly clear as
to Christ's law for His Church. We recognise that
the State has to legislate for all sorts of citizens.
Our plea is (1) that the Church shall be enabled
to claim the observance of its own law by its own
members, and that (2) experience shows the relaxation
of marriage and the extension of divorce to be
contrary to the best interests of the nation. If the
country professes to be Christian it must pay some
regard to Christ's teaching: even if the nation has
ceased to be Christian it may be strongly argued
that a high ideal of marriage is conducive to social
stability and, in the long run, to human happiness.

The parish priest cannot be content with the
negative side of the question. There is great need
of clear, positive, and constructive teaching about
marriage, and no one is qualified to give it unless
he has carefully studied the whole subject. Every
one is conscious of the dangers which beset sex
questions, and it is easy enough to see the disasters
which come from hasty marriages. But there is need

[1] St. Matt. xix. 9.
[2] Divorce means a dissolution of the marriage bond, which
allows either party to "re-marry."

of much knowledge and of still more grace if we are to treat the matter wisely and courageously.[1]

We want our boys and girls to understand that the body is a sacred thing and that no bodily impulse is evil in itself, but that all desires and passions must be kept in check, and made subject to the laws which a loving God has laid down for us: we must help them to think rightly about love and courtship and marriage: there is not one of them but can understand the difference between love and lust. Let us try and show them that marriage is a pure and holy thing, and that in every true marriage the sexual passion, which has its rightful place, will be subject to loyal and unselfish affection between those whom God has made one. We must not be afraid to make war on those artificial preventives which Christian morals can never tolerate. Of course this is not the same thing as saying that there should be no limit to a family. On the contrary, every man, who is a man, will be ready to exercise self-control. But there is such a thing as race-suicide, and the Christian Church will be false to its duty if it does not give its grave warning against practices which are a degradation of marriage and destruction to the home.[2]

Teaching on these difficult subjects is best given by men to men, by women to women. The Church of England Men's Society will help us to sustain a strong public opinion among the men; the Mothers' Union and the Girls' Friendly Society will give valuable help among the women and girls. It is obvious that a book of this sort cannot do more than touch on a subject which is of absolutely vital importance.

II. **Our Own Homes.**—It is good to set forth in our preaching and teaching the ideal of a Christian

[1] Foerster's "Marriage and the Sex Question" is an excellent book on the subject.

[2] See Rawlinson, "Religious Reality," p. 148.

family. It is better still if we can offer an example of it in our own homes. Doubtless that is why at the ordination of priests the bishop asks, " Will you be diligent to frame and fashion your own selves, and *your families*, according to the Doctrine of Christ ; and to make both yourselves *and them*, as much as in you lieth, wholesome examples and patterns to the flock of Christ ? " [1] Of course the question does not imply that all priests will be married : that is a matter of vocation, and there can be little doubt that many priests can better fulfil their service to the Church if they remain unmarried. But where the priest is a married man, it is difficult to overestimate the importance of the example which his home sets to the parish. And on the whole we may thank God for the splendid influence of many a parson's family in town and country.

Yet the priest, like other men, must be on his guard against what Dean Farrar used to call " the slightly expanded egoism of a narrow and selfish domesticity." The ordinary claims of justice demand that his wife and children should occasionally see him. But he will seldom (at least in a town parish) be able to spend an evening by his own fireside, and he, with his wife, must be prepared to sacrifice some of the amenities of the home in order that men and women of all classes may feel themselves really welcomed within the vicarage walls. We want our people to feel at home in our houses, just as we hope that they will make us at home in theirs.

III. **The Homes of Our People.—Visiting.**—How can we be of service to our people in their homes ? Clearly, by visiting. This important subject ought to have a book to itself [2] ; perhaps I can be of most

[1] A similar question is addressed to those who are to be ordained deacons.

[2] Dean Savage's book on " Pastoral Visitation " (Handbooks for the Clergy, Longmans) is admirable.

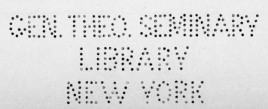

use by offering some very plain advice to my younger brethren who are beginning their ministry.

(1) Do not listen to the plausible but idle clergy who say, "it is not our business to go to the people's homes : it is their business to come to us in Church." This is either slackness or sheer ineptitude. If you neglect the duty of visiting, you will be a mere "idle shepherd," unworthy of your priesthood.

(2) Visit *rich and poor alike*, and let rich and poor alike be treated with scrupulous courtesy and respect. We have no right to force ourselves on anyone, but the great majority of our people (at least in the North and Midlands) will expect us to visit them, and regard us as neglectful if we do not come.

(3) *House to house visiting* is good, but there are special visits which must take precedence. The sick and troubled certainly have first claim. There are families which have given notice of a baptism : absentee teachers or scholars must be looked up. There will, in fact, be a multitude of claims. But avoid the snare of paying frequent and lengthy visits to the people whom you like best at the expense of less pleasant parishioners. All the homes in your district have a claim on you. It is a good thing at special periods—*e.g.*, a parochial mission—to make a concentrated effort to visit the whole parish.

(4) As to the *time of visiting*—the afternoon is generally best. But it is very important to reserve at least one evening a week for visiting the men. Common sense and common courtesy will keep you from calling when you are obviously not wanted, *e.g.*, at meal times or on washing day.

(5) *How are we to be of spiritual service?*—How shall we save our visits from being the occasion for a mere exchange of civilities? This is a real difficulty to many good priests. As with many other problems, the solution to it depends on what sort of men we are. Bishop Wilkinson never visited any

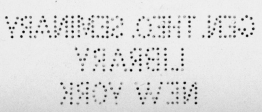

house, whether in a slum or in Eaton Square, without saying a prayer: but then he was Bishop Wilkinson, and it was the simple natural thing for him to do. We must aim at living so near to God that it is perfectly natural to us to speak to our people about Him. But we must not be unreal, nor must we force "religious conversation" on our people. At a first visit we shall probably be content to establish a friendly relationship. Then we shall watch for our opportunity, and we must not be cowardly in shirking it when it comes. And the opportunity will come sure enough if we make it our practice to pray for each family, before and after we visit them.

(6) Have a *regular system* in your visiting. Keep a register of all the families in your district (a "card register" is perhaps best). Of course you will not make notes while you are visiting, but will be careful to write up the register when you get home. If you make private notes about the character of your people, take care that they are kept private. And let it be a point of honour with you that when you leave the parish your successor shall have complete information about your district.[1]

(7) The *visitation of the sick* is one of our greatest privileges and opportunities. In no part of our work is there greater need for the delicacy of perception, the loving sympathy, the spiritual courage which mark a true priest. It is impossible to lay down any general rules. The office for the visitation of

[1] When one is new to a district, one can find the names of the people in the municipal list of electors. The particulars which one needs on the register are obvious enough. (1) Members of the family. (2) Church or chapel. (3) Names of children and what schools they attend, week-day and Sunday. (4) Trade of father. (5) Any communicants? Any candidates for confirmation? It need hardly be said that the information will be gradually and naturally obtained : no priest would be so foolish as to fire off a series of questions.

the sick, though it can seldom if ever be used in its entirety, gives us invaluable guidance ; it points to those old paths of penitence and faith along which the sick person should be gently led : some of the prayers in it are quite perfect.

There are books which give useful help,[1] but a priest must learn to do without any book at the bedside. He must know how to pray in the simplest words. His memory should be stored with passages from the Bible and with some of the well-known hymns. Sometimes it is good to tell a Bible story in one's own words. I have vivid recollection of being called to visit a dying woman, the wife of a publican. Something moved me to tell her the story of the Cross in my own words : then I said, "Of course, you have often heard that story before." She answered, "No, sir, I cannot remember hearing it." That gave me the opportunity, and I hope the poor woman learnt to know something of the love of our crucified Lord, and to put her trust in Him.

Obviously there is need of different treatment for different cases. Here are a few examples :—

(*a*) You are called in suddenly to visit a dying man whom you do not know. On your way you will find out all you can from your messenger. Perhaps when you arrive you find him *in articulo mortis* : you can do little else than say a fervent prayer and set before him the Cross of our Lord Jesus Christ. Perhaps he lives for a few days. You will visit him frequently, and it may be necessary, if friends are crowding round, to ask them very courteously to leave you alone with the patient at your next visit ; then you will speak very gently and plainly of God's love, and of the need of keeping nothing back from Him : but you will remember that his poor body is incapable of much effort, and it is essential that you

---

[1] Bishop Walsham How's "Pastor in Parochia" is still one of the best.

should not weary him or cause him to dread your visits. At the end you may feel that you have not done much, but the "Love of God is wider than the measure of man's mind."

Those priests who have had the privilege of serving as chaplains to the forces will have learnt many lessons about ministering to those who are suddenly called to prepare for the passing from this world.

(*b*) You meet with a case of prolonged sickness. Here there is an opportunity for real conversion—if conversion is needed. You will try to make a diagnosis of the man's spiritual condition. There may be mountains of ignorance to overcome or morasses of prejudice to bridge over. You will not be in a hurry : unobtrusive and thoughtful practical kindness will often do much to remove obstacles. In many cases you will find that preparation of the patient for Holy Communion offers a good objective. It gives the opportunity for the simplest teaching about Christian faith and practice, and if, after your help and guidance, he is desirous to make his communion, it will be perfectly natural to move the sick person to "make a special confession of his sins if he feels his conscience troubled by any weighty matter." If he is unconfirmed, the bishop will be glad when he is in the neighbourhood to come and confirm him. Where this is impossible, he will certainly be "ready and desirous to be confirmed," and may be admitted to Communion.

(*c*) There are also cases of chronic illness, where an invalid lives on for months, or it may be for years. Among these partners of Christ's sufferings we shall find some of our truest saints, some of our most faithful intercessors. Often we shall learn from them far more than we can teach. We ought to visit them regularly, if possible on a fixed day. It will generally be best to take some continuous course of subjects with them, and we shall always be ready to tell them of persons or causes which need their prayers.[1]

(*d*) There need surely be no controversy as to the careful and reverent use of *Unction*, the oil of healing. It is wholly scriptural:[2] it is a true symbol of the spirit of healing. Many of us have known of cases in which God has wonderfully used it for the restoration of bodily health, and it brings comfort to the suffering and the dying. It is greatly to be desired that this beautiful and significant rite may be restored to more frequent use in our own part of the Church of God.

[1] It ought to be unnecessary to say that infectious cases must never be neglected. Reasonable precautions will be taken, and a priest will be scrupulously careful not to convey infection from one house to another.

[2] St James v. 14.

CHAPTER XI

THE SCHOOL

EVER since our Lord put the "feeding of the lambs" in the forefront of His commission to St. Peter, the pastors of the Church have felt a special responsibility for the spiritual care of the little ones of the flock. We believe that it is right for them to be brought to Him in Holy Baptism, in order that in every part of their life—as infants, as children, as young men and maidens, as well as in mature life—they may be dedicated to Him and may come under the shelter of His grace. But this carries with it the supreme duty of teaching children to know Him and of training them as members of His family. This duty must be shared between the home, the school, and the Church. Nothing can take the place of the influence of a good home : the child who has not learnt to pray at his mother's knees, and has received no help from either father or mother in gaining the best of all knowledge, suffers irreparable loss. We cannot lay upon our schools a burden too heavy for them to bear, and there are functions in which the teacher cannot really be *in loco parentis*.

Nevertheless the school fills a place of increasing importance in the life of the country. There are, alas, many children who learn little enough that is good from their parents, and whom the Church has failed to touch. The one opportunity of helping them is given to the school. Even in happier families the parents, sometimes from a quite false modesty, sometimes because they are conscious of their own ignorance, deliberately leave the moral and spiritual training of their children to the school teachers.

I. **Religious Education.**—Thus the influence of the school is really incalculable, and the clergy are bound to feel the utmost sympathy with the teachers in their momentously important duties, and to qualify themselves to take their own rightful part in the work of religious education.

If we are, as we ought to be, enthusiasts for education, we need to think out our educational ideals. What is education and what are its aims? "The object of education is to assist human beings to become themselves. They cannot become themselves without an effort of mind and will, and the discipline by which that effort is stimulated and guided is education:" "the ultimate object of education is the development of personality." . . . In this quite admirable answer to our question the National Mission Report on Industry brings us on to the highest possible ground. It lifts us clear above the conception of a child's mind as "a vase to be filled," and shows that it is rather "a fire to be kindled." [1] It enforces Ruskin's saying, "It is not education to teach a child the tricks of figures and the shapes of letters, and then leave him to turn his arithmetic to roguery and his literature to lust"; it saves us from the miserably low ideal of educating our children for any self-centred end. For no human personality can ever become perfect in selfish isolation. If the intellect is to be trained to observe accurately and to think clearly; if the conscience is to be enlightened and strengthened; if the affections and the will are to be set resolutely towards that which is good, there must be a purpose that lifts the child above himself and his own ends. He must be trained for the unselfish service of his fellows and

[1] Bishop Knox, "Pastors and Teachers," p. 10,

for following God's will. In other words, education must be religious through and through.

Mr. Clutton Brock's excellent book, "The Ultimate Aim," leads us to the same result by another road. He tells us that the child must be trained to seek truth for truth's sake, to admire the beautiful because it is beautiful, to love the good because it is good. But we cannot well be satisfied until we have gained some end in which truth and beauty and goodness find perfect union. That end is God.

There may be some scheme of pedagogy which is atheistic. It may be possible to train children to be efficient wealth-producers without religion. Such schemes may be interesting, but they are not education. If our ideal is a sound one it is clear that the whole scope of education is of vital interest to the Christian Church, quite apart from the religious instruction which (as we shall see presently) must be a necessary part of it. We ought to be enthusiasts for education simply because every human personality is of infinite value to God, and it must be His will that each of His children should attain to fulness of life and become fit and capable for the most effective service. Therefore we warmly welcome such efforts as our country is making at this moment for a fuller and more enlightened training of the children : we shall sympathise with the demand that there shall not merely be a "ladder" for a few exceptional boys and girls, but a highway of educational progress along which all who are capable of travelling it shall receive the best education which the country can offer, and shall press forward to the complete development of all their powers.

While, however, we believe that all real education must have God for its inspiration and God for its end, and that no subject ought to be "secular," our schemes for the development of children's minds and characters will surely fail if the most important subject of all is left severely alone or regarded as a mere extra. Religious instruction is vital to religious education. What we desire is that our children should know God as revealed in Jesus Christ. In Him alone they can find perfect truth : the splendour of His beauty must win their admiration and their love : to the call of His goodness their conscience must respond —for in Him can be seen the ideal of perfect love and matchless heroism. Those who see Him will see the Father. The aim of religious instruction is to show the children, or rather to enable them to find out for themselves with God's help, the answers to these questions—Who is Jesus Christ ? What does He show us about God and about ourselves ? To what sort of venture does He call us, and what kind of character does He want to see in us ? How can we lift up our hearts to God, and how can we get His power in our lives ? How can we be of use to Him as members of His great family ?

We cannot answer such questions without constant appeal to the Bible. Obviously wherever there is religious instruction there must be " simple Bible teaching." But unhappily it is possible to give Bible teaching which has little or no religion in it. There are cases in which " religious teaching is degraded to the level of unintelligent history teaching ; and there is no subject which can be taught so unintelligently as history." [1] As Bishop Knox puts it, " We have taught too much Jewish history, too little Christian verity." [2] Huppim, Muppim, and Ard have become proverbial, and even New Testament teaching may be arid and distasteful to the children. A certain teacher who gave some lessons on "the execution of Jesus" cannot have shown his scholars much of the glory and mystery of the Cross.

The first necessity for Bible teaching is that it should touch the spiritual life of the children. But

[1] Rev. G. C. Bell, quoted by Bishop Knox, " Pastors and Teachers," p. 51.
[2] " Pastors and Teachers," p. 71.

there are other considerations which are not unimportant. We must not teach the children anything which they will afterwards have to unlearn. Obviously this danger is most likely to occur in the Old Testament lesson. One cannot for a moment depreciate the value of the Old Testament books. But there is need of intelligence as well as reverence in teaching (*e.g.*) the narrative of the creation ; and children ought clearly to understand that we do not look to the Old Testament for that perfect standard of goodness which was made known to us by Jesus Christ : the Old Testament books show us the school in which God was training His people to be ready for the coming of His Son, in Whom all truth, and beauty, and goodness are to be seen.

A careful scheme and plan—a " syllabus," as it is called—is necessary. But it must be abundantly obvious that the effectiveness of religious teaching depends first and last, and always, on the teacher. If the teacher does not know this greatest of all subjects, or, what is even more serious, does not care about it, his instruction may be valueless or even harmful. We may thank God for the large number of earnest and efficient teachers who in every sort of school, secondary as well as primary, Council or Church, have trained generations of children in the knowledge and love of God. The most useful work which the Church can do for religious education is to ensure that every teacher shall have the fullest opportunity of becoming well equipped for this vitally important duty.

II. **The Day School.**—The most important sphere of religious education is the day school ; and the secondary school has, if possible, a greater opportunity than the elementary school. Let us consider what our part is in helping the school to do its work well.

We must recognise, first of all, that the part directly taken by the Church in the guidance of education has greatly diminished during recent years.

The majority of the elementary school children now attend Council schools, and the secondary education of the country has been taken even more completely out of our hands. It is useless for us to complain or to shake our heads over it. For good or for evil— and it need not necessarily be for evil—the State has taken over a great part of the work for human welfare which was once the monopoly of the Church. Quite apart from our Church schools—which, as I shall try to show presently, are of vital importance—our influence on the whole education of the country may be undiminished.

We must first make up our minds not to decry or disparage Council schools. We do not believe in the undenominational principle, but in spite of its cramping limitations there are many Christian teachers in Council schools who lead their children nearer to God. The time is surely ripe for a national declaration of policy in favour of providing effective religious teaching in all schools which are supported by public money, the rights of parents and of teachers being guarded by a conscience clause. Moreover, it might well be recognised that while it is the duty of the State to see that religious teaching is given, the direction of that teaching should be in the hands of the Christian Church, which in this case would mean all Christian communions who are ready to take part in it.[1] Why should not an interdenominational council be established in each area to attend

[1] "The force behind it all (religious education) must be the organised forces of the Churches. It cannot be the organised forces of the ratepayers or of the Department, or of the County Council. Whatever it may be, it cannot be that. It must be the religious force provided by ecclesiastical organisation. . . . As for the idea that because you do not think there is sufficient agreement among the Churches, you are going to make up a sort of bastard State religion, and treat that as if it had behind it the authority of an ecclesiastical organisation : the more it is considered the more absurd it will seem."—From a speech by Mr. A. J. Balfour.

to this important business? Such a plan would imply no sort of distrust of the teachers, who ought indeed to be strongly represented on the council.

It is clearly our duty to use our utmost influence, together with other Christian people, in securing the best possible religious teaching in all the State schools. But we are convinced that the continued existence and increasing vigour of schools directly connected with the Church, or other Christian communions, is really vital to the maintenance of a right standard of religious education. It is surely superfluous to give more than the briefest explanation of our reason for believing in Church schools.

(1) Many of the wisest experts, like Dr. Michael Sadler, assure us that the country would be the poorer if it were deprived of the wealth of initiative, and of the variety of ideals, which are ensured by the presence of different types of schools.

(2) While the religious instruction in Council schools may be, and sometimes is, as good as its limitations permit, there is security in Church schools that Christian ideals shall be kept in the forefront of all the work of education.

(3) Above all, the Church school is able to treat the child not merely as an individual Christian, but as a member of the Christian family. He can receive a full training in that vital religion which will enable him to take his part, strengthened by the grace of God, in the great sacrament of fellowship, in the worship and work of God, and in useful service to his fellows.

From the point of view of the parish priest, there is all the difference in the world between a parish which has a Church school and one which has none. In the one case he can soon get to know all the children, and has priceless opportunities of influence, in the other all kinds of resourceful efforts have to be made before he can even begin the work of " feeding the lambs."

8

What part can a parish priest take in a Church day school? First of all he will make friends with the teachers. He will show respect for them and sympathy with them. Even if he is already armed with experience, he will learn from them lessons in the teacher's craft which will be of lasting value. The last thing which he will dream of is to patronise them. Let us be honest and confess that some clergy have missed golden opportunities, and have even done serious mischief by failing to honour the teacher as a fellow-worker in God's kingdom. Presently we shall have cause to speak of help which the Church ought to give in the equipment of teachers for the work of religious instruction.

Of course the clergy will pay frequent visits to the school. A deacon or young priest who knows little about teaching[1] will frankly confess that he is a learner, and will listen and observe before he begins to teach. When he is called on to take a class he will fall in with the general scheme, and accept whatever work is assigned to him. He will teach, not deliver homilies: that is to say, he must appeal to the intellect of the children; but he will not be satisfied with obtaining accurate repetition of formulas or cramming the memory with facts. It is essential that the children should be interested in what they learn, that they should be led to think about it, and to care for it.

A passage in Bishop Gott's excellent " Parish Priest of the Town " is illuminating:[2] " The first task set to a new curate by the schoolmaster is the preparation of the children for the next religious examination. I suppose you must try your best with it, but your best leaves it still nothing nobler than a task set you

[1] It is greatly to be desired that the art of teaching should be among the subjects in which clergy are trained before ordination.

[2] p. 26.

by a schoolmaster. The better you succeed, the surer and deeper is your failure. For a competitive examination, especially a religious one, is the most unspiritual occupation of a mind. Inspiration and cram are as contrary, the one to the other, as the spirit and the flesh ; and as the inspector leaves your class, either the master will look at you with disgust and contempt, or your priestly conscience will condemn you for making merchandise of the grace of God."

This is really a most damning indictment of a whole system, which one hopes is becoming rapidly extinct. Where the religious "inspection" is of this sort the curate is well advised to disregard it. But why should the teachers be condemned to such a soul-destroying drill? And why should we tolerate a method which has long been discarded in "secular" subjects as contrary to all educational principles? Happily there are now many dioceses where the inspector, coming as the friend and counsellor of clergy and teachers, is able to test the reality and reverence of the religious influence and instruction without any recourse to methods which inevitably degrade the teacher and mislead the child.

Once again let us remember that the supreme subject of our teaching is God revealed in Jesus Christ, and that our purpose is to enable our children to know Him and to love Him so that they may take their right place in His family, and be ready for worship and for war.

The privilege of worship can only be understood by practice. It is good that the children who are members of our Church should from time to time come to a short service in the church during the hour set apart for religious instruction. The teachers will give their cordial help. Where there is no Church school, arrangements can often be made for the children in Council schools to attend church on special Holy Days.[1]

III. The Training of the Teacher.—I make no apology for returning to the all-important subject of the training of the teacher. It is really the key to the whole position. Ingenious schemes and elaborate syllabuses are utterly useless unless the teachers care about religious teaching and are qualified to give it.

Let us first remember that the teaching profession is a branch of the Civil Service. Therefore there can be no religious "tests" for teachers. Parents have a right to demand that their children shall be trained in religious knowledge by teachers who believe what they teach. But the community cannot refuse even an atheist full access to the teaching profession.

We must further recognise that teachers—as represented, let us say, by their strong trade union—are by no means disposed to accept anything which they would call interference. And indeed they are justified in requiring that they should be taken into fullest counsel with regard to any scheme which touches their life and work. But the Church—by which I here mean the organised Christian communions—ought to have a strong say in the religious upbringing of Christian children, and (if there is no fear of "dictation") the teachers, as well as the public educational authorities, will be wise enough to welcome the help which the Church alone can give in the religious training of the teachers. How can this help be given?

(1) It is absolutely vital that our Church should retain and strengthen the Church Training Colleges. It is impossible to estimate the debt which the country owes to them. It is to these colleges that we must look for the maintenance of the highest possible ideals of Christian education.

---

[1] This "right of exodus" is secured in those educational areas where the L.E.A. has adopted the Anson by-law. It is greatly to be desired that this by-law should be universally applied.

But we have to face the fact that an increasing number of teachers are being trained in colleges established by County Councils or by Universities. Is it too much to ask that full opportunity, and sufficient time should be given to all the students for receiving the equipment which shall enable them to give religious instruction? Many of them will be called on, and will desire, to give such teaching in their future schools. No self-respecting teacher cares to teach a subject which he does not know. Apart from the work done within the college, the authorities will as a rule offer facilities for the students to attend classes organised by our Church for our own members, provided that the instruction is undertaken by a really qualified teacher.

(2) We must do our best to help the future teachers at an earlier stage. In every deanery classes should be organised for student teachers, and for those pupils in the secondary schools who are intending to enter the teaching profession. It is not at all an easy business, and everything will depend on the personality of the men or women who take the classes in hand. May we not add that it is clearly our duty to set before our best boys and girls the splendid opportunities for useful service in God's kingdom which the work of a teacher will afford them? It is a great vocation, second only to one other.

(3) Why should not lectures and classes be organised in convenient centres for the fuller equipment of the teachers? There is a large and growing number of teachers who would warmly welcome such help.

IV. **The Sunday School.**—We turn from the day school to the Sunday school. Here at least we have a perfectly free hand. If the opportunity of Sunday teaching had been fully bought up, what a splendid company of worshipping, witnessing, working members the Church might possess! It is clear enough that in our Sunday schools we have left undone some of the things which we ought to have done.

The strong point in our Sunday schools has been the personal influence of good men and women on generations of boys and girls. Since the rationale of the Sunday school is a closer spiritual touch and more direct appeal than is possible in the day school, this personal asset is of untold value. But the weakness of the average Sunday school has been bad discipline, defective teaching, and miserable equipment. We cannot fairly blame the teachers: in many cases we have not given them a chance. We have failed to understand that good educational methods are the same everywhere, and that we dishonour God if we neglect to apply the best possible means for the training of His children as members of His family. There is nothing spiritual about disorder and ineffective teaching.

Again we are brought back to the truism that everything depends on the training of the teacher. The difficulties are enormous; in most parishes the teachers are very busy people, and some of those whose spiritual influence is strongest have never had the advantage of thorough education. But if they are offered really first-rate training and instruction they will be glad enough to give up their scanty leisure. There is need for training in educational principles as well as for instruction in the subjects which they will be asked to teach. Here is a work for the clergy which is of intense interest and unspeakable importance. It should be assigned to the best man on the staff, and he ought to take infinite trouble with it. When one hears that "teachers will not come to the preparation class," it very often means that it is not worth their while to come; they do not profit much from an ill-prepared and undigested summary of next Sunday's lesson.

Is not this training of teachers a sphere in which combined interparochial action may be possible? No doubt a priest rightly values the opportunity which the teacher's class gives him for close contact

with his best workers. But at least the training in
good teaching methods might be given in combined
classes. Where there is a good Sunday School
Teachers' Association (and there should be one in
every deanery) a training week for Sunday school
teachers, conducted by an expert from the National
Society, or the Sunday School Institute, has proved
to be of great value. I have very happy recollections
of a course of lectures given at Liverpool by Canon
Morley Stevenson on child nature and the art of
teaching; they were organised by an Interdenominational Committee in which other Christian
communions joined—and why should not all Christian teachers combine for such a purpose?

The better training of teachers is part of a movement for Sunday school reform which began several
years ago, but which has by no means finished its
work.[1] All who have entered into this movement
know that it puts the first thing first, and that its
supreme aim is the spiritual life of children—their
fellowship with God in Jesus Christ, and their development as worshipping and working members of
His family. It tries to reach this end by adapting
to the Sunday school those methods which science
and experience have proved to be sound.

The subject should be studied in some of the
excellent books which deal with it; and a parish
priest who wishes to improve his Sunday school
would do well to visit some parish where reformed
methods are in good working order. Very briefly,
the main principles of Sunday school reform are:
(1) The grading of the scholars; (2) Self-expression;
(3) Proper equipment.

(1) *Grading of Scholars.*—Different subjects and
different methods are obviously needed for different
children. Most of us have attempted the task of
teaching (probably in Church) a mixed multitude

[1] See Report of Archbishop's Committee on Sunday school
reform (S.P.C.K).

of children of ages varying, say, from 6 to 16; if we think that we have succeeded, we grossly deceive ourselves.

In a good-sized Sunday school *at least* four grades are needed. (*a*) The junior school, up to and including 7 years old; (*b*) the lower middle school, 8-10; (*c*) the upper middle school, 11-13; (*d*) the senior school, 14 and upwards. These age limits, of course, are not rigid.

(*a*) The junior school should be in charge of a skilled teacher, preferably a trained infant-school teacher, who understands the best methods of teaching young children. She may be assisted by a large number of young "helpers," consisting of the ablest and keenest boys and girls of 14 and upwards, each of whom takes charge, for part of the school time, of four or five children, while they all attend a weekly class of instruction and training. This class of "helpers" is an excellent recruiting ground for future Sunday school teachers.

(*b*) and (*c*). The middle departments need careful superintendence. The time will be more broken up than in an ancient Sunday school (very few teachers can secure attention for a forty minutes' continuous lesson), and the better adaptation of subjects to the children's minds will secure greater interest, and therefore better discipline.

(*d*) In most parts of England, except Lancashire, the senior school will consist chiefly of Bible classes. Every one knows that the classes for big lads offer one of the most important bits of work in the parish, and quite the most difficult.

(2) *Self-Expression.*—Our purpose is not merely to pour information into the children's memories, but to help them to ask questions, to observe, and to think. Doubtless we want them to know the Christian faith. But they will not know it or remember it unless they are interested in it and care about it, and this interest will never be secured if their minds are merely passive

and receptive. Self-expression means their active co-operation in the business of learning. With little children it may take the form of drawing pictures of some object suggested by the lesson. Older children may have note-books in which they can write out some of the main points of the lesson. If they learn how to worship God well, one of the best forms of self-expression will have been reached.

(3) *Equipment.*—It is obvious that considerable expenditure on equipment will be necessary. In the junior school, ingenuity will make a small apparatus go a long way : in the lower middle school, pictures are almost a necessity : the upper middle school must have note-books. There is no reason why, where there is a Church day school, there should not be common use of at least some of the accessories. But there is also no reason why the Sunday school should be starved, and where the school itself attracts scholars, as a well-ordered and interesting school always will, there is the less need to spend money on "prizes" for scholars.[1]

This whole method of reform is difficult, but I know from personal experience that it is not impossible. In a certain large parish, with the help of excellent colleagues, I tried the plan and found that it made an untold difference to the whole parish. Of course we took the teachers into consultation ; they warmly supported the scheme, and after a few months' experience they would not for worlds have gone back to the old system, or want of system. We began with the junior department, and a year later we took the middle school in hand, converting the upper middle school (children of about 10-13) into a catechism which met on Sunday afternoons in church. Three teachers' training classes were necessary each week, one for each grade. The result of the reform was that our school greatly increased in numbers,

---

[1] I will not suggest economising on the children's annual excursion, which is a priceless boon for many poor children.

and (what was far more important) the whole discipline and tone of it were transformed. The children were keen about their work, and the Sunday school became a joy instead of a burden.

One result of the reform in the Sunday school is that teachers are far more easily obtained. Men and women who would not feel it worth while to spend a toilsome Sunday afternoon in a disorderly and badly organised school are glad to help where there really is a chance of useful and interesting teaching.

There is one other change in method which is most desirable, but which I frankly admit I have never accomplished. Where there is a Church day school it is most unreasonable that the Sunday school should be no more closely related to it than if the two were on different planets. Why should not one scheme and syllabus be devised in which each should take its part?[1]

V. The Catechism.—I have left till last the plan of religious instruction which is in some ways the most promising of all—*i.e.*, the method of St. Sulpice, commonly called the "catechism." It is too well-known to need description. Every one should read Bishop Dupanloup's "Ministry of Catechising." The method is educationally sound. The children are graded; the whole complex of the child's mind is appealed to—memory, reason, affections, conscience, and will; there is ample opportunity for self-expression, the "analysis" of the instruction being particularly useful; the variety of exercises helps to secure attention, and the care of detail in the arrangement of the children and in the appointment of officers from the children themselves tends to promote order and reverence. There is no reason why the creation of a catechism should involve the abolition of Sunday school; it is surely the best plan to confine the catechism to one department of the

[1] The National Society have planned out an admirable scheme of the kind.

school—say the children between ten and fourteen. It will then offer a useful opportunity for the special training which immediately precedes and follows confirmation.

In parishes where there is no Church day school, it is sometimes useful to establish a catechism on some week day.

There are a few warnings which experience shows to be necessary.

(1) The catechism is a great strain on the priest who conducts it, and it requires an immense amount of time and pains in the preparation for the various exercises, and in looking over the analyses afterwards. There is no reason why a layman or a laywoman should not take a prominent part in the catechising. (2) The memory work is the least important part of the catechism. The mere answering of set questions is of very little use by itself. The instruction and "homily" are far more useful. (3) It is a grave mistake to mass together in one catechism children of very different ages.

One word must be added to this already lengthy chapter. It is essential to all religious education that children should be trained in the life of worship and of service which belongs to the Christian family. Devout and reverent worship can only be learnt by practice ; when children come to church, care should be taken that they are so placed that they can really take part in the service, and above all things church-going must not be made a burden to them. As to the life of service, children can learn at a very early age to be kind and helpful, and the cause of missions should constantly be set before them, as the warfare which the Church is waging at many fronts. We must be bad teachers indeed if we cannot impart to them something of the thrill of this great campaign of God's kingdom, so that they desire to take some part in the venture to which our Leader calls us.

CHAPTER XII

ORGANISATION OF A PARISH

ORGANISATION is not the first thing needed. The Church of Sardis, to which the risen Lord said, "I know thy works, that thou hast a name that thou livest and art dead,"[1] was probably a very well-organised community. The first need is the presence and power of the Spirit and Life-giver. The most excellently devised machinery is useless unless there is the power to work it.

Seeing, however, that we are called to be God's fellow-workers, we shall dishonour Him unless we use the best means within our reach for painstaking and effective service. Therefore we must organise, for civilised man is an organising animal, and, just as in the great war a single well-planned organisation, the outward embodiment of the united purpose of the allied nations, has been the essential condition of victory, so the Church of God ought to think out its plan of campaign, and make the most skilful use of all its resources in order that it may fight under the Captain of our Salvation, not as a disorderly mass of guerilla bandits, but "terrible as an army with banners," disciplined and organised for the campaign against the powers of darkness.

We are often told that we need less organisation : so indeed we do, if it is the futile and ineffective organisation with which we are sometimes saddled. But let it be understood that good organisation does

[1] Rev. iii. 1.

not add to our work, but makes it go the furthest possible way. Good organisation does not take the place of personal influence—nothing can—but enables us to extend our personal influence to its utmost capacity.

The limitations of this chapter are obvious. Not only must we confine ourselves almost entirely to the unit of the parish, leaving on one side the diocese and the church as a whole, but we have to recognise that parishes are of infinite variety, and that no one scheme could possibly apply to all. Let us content ourselves with a few general principles.

I. **Keep the Purpose in View.**—It is not our aim to make the parish a successful going concern, any more than it is the Church's aim to be a powerful and imposing corporation. Our aim—as we have said already—is *missionary*. Our work is for the conversion of men to God, so that all the members of the flock "may have life and may have it abundantly." But while our burning desire is to win to God all the people of the parish and to build them up as living stones in the fellowship of His Church, we shall soon find that our efforts will fail if we set any limits to our missionary purpose.

Narrowness of outlook is ruinous to spiritual vitality. Our desire for the conversion of souls must go out in ever-widening circles. We must pray and work for God's kingdom in our village or town, in our diocese, in our country, in our Empire, throughout the whole world. In the parish which cares nothing for the work of the diocese or for missions overseas you will not hear of many conversions. It is very difficult to understand how a priest and his communicants can be complacently contented to send £20 a year to missions, while they spend £200 on the luxuries of their church.

All the organisations of the parish itself will find their true proportion if the missionary purpose is kept steadily in view. Our arrangements for the reverent worship of God; educational work in day and Sunday schools and among adults; schemes for the special care of children, and for looking after the best interests of lads and girls; temperance and purity work; schemes for social welfare; even the provision for recreation and kindly intercourse—all will serve the one end. One example will suffice by way of illustration: clubs for men or for lads and for girls may seem to be "secular," and may not produce direct and immediate spiritual results: they will certainly not "bring men to church" all at once; but they ought to lead to a spirit of fellowship, they provide fuller and more human interests, and, as part of our whole scheme, conduce to the recognition of God's sovereignty over every side of our common life.

II. **Trust the Laity.**—The example which we have just given also illustrates the necessity of enlisting the aid of the laity. The clergy cannot and ought not to give a great deal of their time to clubs and social work. This is plainly the business of the laymen and women of the parish—one of the many spheres in which their active and constant help is indispensable. At many points in this book we have been led to emphasise the fact that the progress of the Church depends on the witness and the work of the whole body. In evangelisation, in teaching, in visitation, in social reform of all kinds, men and women of all classes will set their minds and hands to the work. But the laity cannot be expected to do their best work if the parson persists in "running the parish" as absolute monarch. They must be treated as partners, with a really effective voice in the management of what is the most important business in the world. It is true that we have to pay the price of clerical autocracy and lay apathy in past years. A capable priest may feel that the

work would be better done under his sole direction :
so very likely it would—at first.   But the real secret
of democracy lies in the fact that responsibility is
the greatest educative force in the world.   In the
long run we shall find that the more responsibility
and managing power we place on the shoulders of
the laity, the better will the work of the parish be
done.   Again one illustration will suffice.   It has
been decided, let us say, to arrange a service for men,
weekly or monthly.   The priest will be wise if he
entrusts the whole management of it to a committee
of the men, probably the executive of the C.E.M.S.
in the parish.   They may make some mistakes, but
in the end the service will fulfil its purpose far more
effectively than if the parson kept the arrangements
in his own hands.

The best opportunity of trusting the laity is afforded
by the Church Council for the parish.   Many parishes
in town and country already possess one, and rejoice
in the possession.   Before long, if the proposals of
the Church and State Committee take effect, there
will be a statutory Church Council in every parish.
At the time of writing this chapter, the question of
constitution is still uncertain.   We may be quite sure
that membership in the council will be confined to
communicants, including women.   The conditions of
franchise are, at the moment, a subject of acute controversy.   But I am perfectly certain that a parish
council, well and wisely conducted, will be a immense source of strength to the parish.

Some of the clergy are apprehensive as to the
result of such a council, for two quite different
reasons.   Some fear that the council will be a drag
on the advance of parish work, a wet blanket which
will stifle progress.   My own experience is quite to
the contrary.   I have clear recollections of a parish
in Lancashire in which a mission church was greatly
needed for a populous outlying district.   As vicar, I

counselled delay on the ground that the parish had incurred heavy expenditure on other enterprises ; the parish council, however, took the bit between their teeth, and insisted on immediate action ; and they saw the business through.

Others are afraid lest the parish council should assume authority in determining the doctrine that shall be preached, and the ceremonial which shall be used, in the church. It would clearly be preposterous for rules of doctrine or devotion to be laid down by the mere majority of a parish council. The priest cannot delegate his authority in such matters. But it is surely right that the representatives of the laity should give their consent before the hours and plans of worship are changed. The council will be a support and not a hindrance to any parish priest who wishes to lead his flock rather than to drive them ; it will often prove a strong safeguard against noisy and quite ungodly minorities, who might otherwise make his life a burden. It may possibly be argued that some changes in our Church customs, which are, by common confession, an improvement on past methods, would not have come to pass if the consent of parish councils had been necessary. There might have been some delay, but surely in the long run the position would have been more secure.

One bit of work which will be controlled by the parish council is the direction of parochial finance. Every wise parish priest leaves money matters, as far as he possibly can, in the hands of the laity. The relations between the churchwardens and the parish council may require careful handling ; but, speaking generally, the responsibility for raising money, and the determination of the directions in which it shall be spent, should rest with the council : if the members of the council have a real share in the work of the parish for the kingdom of God, there will be less fear of their attempting to apply " commercial " principles of the baser sort to the support of spiritual work. In most parishes the " free-will offering " scheme has been found the best means of providing the sinews of war : the principle of it is that every communicant shall give regularly (by weekly instalments if necessary) for the support of the church : here, as always, success will largely depend on the efficiency of the secretary, but a good parish council will consider it a point of honour to make the scheme effectual in providing for the parochial quota to the diocesan fund, and for the efficient working of the parish agencies. For special purposes a sale of work or bazaar (of course without raffles or other such abominations) may be necessary, but experience shows that faithful and systematic giving can become a real fruit of the spiritual life of the people of a parish.[1]

III. **Work from a Centre.**—Where the laity are trusted, the most reliable and efficient men and women will surely come to the fore. The communicants are the natural rallying point for the whole parish, and the Communicants' Guild should be, as it were, a central power-station for all spiritual work. Among the communicants there will be some tried and faithful workers who will be the right-hand men (and women) of the clergy in evangelistic, educational, and social enterprises. No time is wasted which is spent on the training of teachers and visitors. History constantly repeats itself, and every religious movement has started from a strong central body of men and women who were on fire with the Spirit of God, and ready to take any amount of pains to become His efficient instruments in the work of the kingdom.

IV. **Follow after Unity.**—If the communicants are a real red-hot centre to the parish, the sacrament of fellowship ought to secure unity among the

[1] Here the mission field has something to teach us. The Archdeacon of Lebombo writes :—" Every Lebombo Christian is assessed for God's work as a natural and necessary part of the good management of the church, and what is really significant is that in public worship the heathen are requested to leave before the collection. Giving to God is regarded as a Christian privilege which those who are not of the family cannot claim."

9

brethren. But since the early days of the Church of Corinth, divisions have been the curse of every ecclesia. The causes are various. Sometimes schisms arise from ecclesiastical partizanship; more frequently they are the result of mere personal jealousies or social snobbishness; sometimes, alas, the Paul[1] party and Apollos party are reproduced in the parties of the vicar and the curate—smaller men than Paul and Apollos—while the " Christ party" is seldom wanting, being represented by the people who claim the possession of Christ as their monopoly.

The cure for these troubles does not come within the scope of this chapter. The only remedy is more real conversion. But there is one frequent cause of schism which belongs to the organisation of the parish—namely the mission church. " Corruptio optimi pessima": the mission church may be one of the brightest spots in the place, a real centre of spiritual life and brotherly good-will: it may be a curse to the parish.

Mission churches are of two kinds: (1) There is the church which serves a separate district of a large parish: either it is an embryo parish church which may some day form the centre of a new parish; or it forms a unit in some large area which is worked under one head. In either case it will be under the charge of an assistant curate. But there is need of constant intercourse between the clergy and the workers of the whole parish, and of loyal adherence, on all hands, to certain clearly understood principles of worship and work. Else there will be jealousies and misunderstandings: the officials of the mother church will grudgingly give a step-daughter's portion to the district churches, and the congregations of the latter will return the ill-will with interest. I have even known of cases where the vicar of the parish has been regarded as an unwelcome intruder in the district churches.[2]

---

[1] I Cor. iii. 1-9.

[2] One very interesting question of organisation cannot be properly treated here. Is it wise to split up a big parish and form a new parish whenever the growing population justifies it?

(2) Sometimes a mission church is, or ought to be, a centre of evangelistic work and a training ground for those who are only beginning to understand the principles of Church life. It best fulfils its purpose when it sends a perpetual stream of new communicants to the parish church. The situation often becomes difficult; those who found their first knowledge of God in the mission church do not want to leave it; that is right enough, but there is often a tendency to form a little clique which takes possession of the place and is not very cordial to newcomers. Perhaps the curate who is placed in charge is not strong enough to resist the persuasion of those who want to go "one better" than the parish church with a surpliced choir, more florid music, more elaborate ceremonial, and all the rest of it; and having been given a free hand by his vicar he may be tempted merely to indulge his own liturgical fancies and to forget altogether that his purpose in the mission church is to win souls to God. The result is almost sure to be schism; and the mission church will become a weakness rather than a strength in God's work.

V. Avoid Parochialism.—Unity within the parish is good : but it is better still to have unity throughout the Church in each centre of population—in every town or rural district. The Church ought to be able to speak with one voice, to act as one family, to fight

---

Or should a large area, containing several churches, be worked as one whole under one head? The policy of the Ecclesiastical Commissioners on the whole favours the former plan, which doubtless has the advantage of enlisting local enthusiasm. The drawback is that a town may be split up into a number of weak and struggling parishes, no one of which is really able to maintain a vigorous organisation of its own. Good examples of the large parish plan are to be found in Portsea, Yarmouth, Helmsley, Stoke-on-Trent. With the necessary proviso that a first-rate man is to be found to take the helm, I believe this plan to be the best. It certainly lends itself to that concentration, together with the assignment of special men to special duties, which are secrets of good organisation. Where the small parish plan is adopted, it is absolutely necessary that there should be close and friendly co-operation between the parishes in one area.

as one army. The British Navy would not keep the seas clear if the captain of each ship sailed his own course without regard to the other vessels in the squadron; a regiment in the army will not do much in beating the enemy if its own prestige is everything to it, and it recks nothing of its appointed place in the brigade, the division, and the army.

The parish system has much that is good in it. It is good that every person in the country should be able to claim the ministrations of a priest of our Church, and that every priest should feel himself responsible for all the people within his parish who do not refuse his aid. It is good that the priest and people should be keen about their parish, and should passionately desire that its worship and work should be as good and worthy as they know how to make them. There is a proper parish pride as there is a proper regimental pride. But it is futile to demand, in a free country, that every person should, as a matter of duty, attend his parish church. A parish priest ought to be glad to find regular communicants in his parish, whether they attend their parish church or prefer another. On the other hand, a priest is a poor catholic and a bad evangelical if he lays himself out to attract people from other parishes. Nothing can be worse than that the churches of a town should be like a number of independent shops each touting for its neighbour's custom.

There ought, on the contrary, to be the closest unity of action among the parishes of a town or a deanery. Differences of ecclesiastical outlook are not a bar to unity in purpose and policy, or (what is more important) to association in prayer. At the time of the National Mission message I was in close touch with several towns wherein the various parishes represented almost acute differences of teaching and practice, but where all the clergy met for united prayer (in the case of one town making their corporate communion at the different churches in turn), and followed a well-considered plan for concerted action. In another town all the parishes combined in promoting a week's campaign on behalf of purity of life. It is needless to multiply instances. It is not only desirable, but necessary, that the Church in a town or district should give a united witness on the great questions which touch the moral and spiritual welfare of the people. There are many educational enterprises, *e.g.*, the organising of lectures on Christian doctrine and history, the provision of tutorial classes, the training of teachers, etc., which can best be carried through by a combined effort.

Unity among ourselves must come first ; but every Christian man will be desirous of promoting unity with other Christians. It must always be possible and desirable for all Christian people to unite for the promotion of social and moral well-being. Strong witness on behalf of temperance and purity, efforts for social justice and reform of crying abuses, work for infant welfare, are examples which at once come to mind. In all these things we can work and act as if we were one : indeed we are one in this application of our Christianity. Moreover, we have been learning lately that without any sacrifice of principle on either side we can meet our fellow-Christians on some common ground, for united intercession and thanksgiving.

Here then are some principles of good organisation : let priest and people keep the end clear in view ; let them be partners in the great enterprise, working in mutual confidence ; let them keep the central fire strongly burning ; let them do all in their power to promote united action within the parish and beyond it ; and then, by the use of sanctified common sense, and that blending of accurate thinking with bold venture which makes good " business," they will be able to set up good and useful machinery for the enterprise to which they are called, remembering all the time that they must have the " Spirit within the wheels " which will enable the work to go straightforward.[1]

[1] Ezekiel i. 12, 20.

APPENDIX TO CHAPTER XII

SOME PAROCHIAL AND RURIDECANAL ORGANISATIONS [1]

THE following list of organisations can, of course, lay no claim to completeness. On the other hand, it goes without saying that no one parish could attempt to make use of all these organisations. For some items in the list a bare mention is sufficient; in other cases a few comments seem desirable.

I. Parochial.

A. CENTRAL.

(1) *Officers of the Church.*—Churchwardens and synodsmen. For the duties and status of church-wardens, see P. V. Smith.

(2) *Parish Council.*—A constitution for a Parish Council is suggested in the Report of the Archbishop's Committee on Church and State, p. 46 ff.

(3) *Communicants' Guilds.* — See Chapter VIII. Parochial retreats, days of intercession, etc., can be organised through the Guilds.

B. THE WORSHIP OF THE CHURCH.

(1) *Lay Readers.*
(2) *Choirs.*
(3) *Bell-Ringers.*
(4) *Servers' Guilds.*

[1] On this subject, see C. F. Garbett, "Work of a Great Parish" (Longmans).

C. Evangelistic and Pastoral.

(1) *Lay evangelists and women messengers.*

(2) *Visitors.*—Visitors need not be of a "superior class," and in many parishes there are men visitors (often supplied by C.E.M.S.) as well as women visitors. The character of their work and influence will obviously depend on their gifts and training. Some visitors can give direct spiritual help; all can show brotherly or sisterly good-will, and can keep the parish priest informed as to cases of sickness, etc. *Periodic meetings* of visitors are desirable; Bishop Wilkinson's "Spiritual Counsels to District Visitors" (Mowbrays) gives an example of what can be done at such meetings.

The *relief of poverty* should *not* be a part of a visitor's functions.

(3) Some parishioners who do not feel equal to the work of a visitor will often serve as distributors of the *Parish Magazine*, which may be of untold value, especially if it does not confine itself to merely parochial events, but touches on subjects of real importance to the Church and the nation.

(4) *Missionary Association.*—In many parishes it is desirable to band together those who are interested in missionary work. If different people are specially attached to some particular agency (C.M.S., or S.P.G., or U.M.C.A., or some Home Mission Society), it is all the more desirable that they should be brought together. The whole body should be missionaries for missionary work throughout the parish. Sometimes parochial missionary boxes are circulated which can either be allocated, at the holder's desire, to some particular mission, or can be assigned to the general fund, the various destinations of which are determined by the association.

For the children a branch of *King's Messengers* or *Sower's Band* will be useful.

D. EDUCATIONAL.

(1) *Church Day School.*

(2) *Week Day Classes or Catechisms* for children are specially useful where there is no Church day school.

Prayer Circles for Children may be held in an aisle of the church, and need not necessarily be conducted by a priest.

(3) *Sunday Schools and Catechism.*—See Chapter XI.

(4) *Bible Classes.*

(5) *Study Circles.*—Some of the " Student Christian movement " literature will be found useful.

(6) *Tutorial Classes.*

N.B.—It would be well to make an effort to co-ordinate all the *work among children*, Sunday School, Day School, Band of Hope, Missionary Guild, Prayer Circles, etc.

E. SOCIAL AND MORAL.

(1) *Purity.*—A branch of the White Cross League (Headquarters, 7 Dean's Yard, Westminster, S.W.1).

(Rescue and preventive work is better worked in a larger area than that of the parish.)

(2) *Temperance.*—A branch of the C.E.T.S. (Head-quarters, C.E.T.S. House, 50 Marsham Street, West-minster, S.W.1).

(3) Study of social and industrial questions and work for social reform are considered under Ruri-decanal organisations.

F. SOCIAL AND RECREATIONAL.

Clubs for men, for lads, and for girls are almost a necessity in town parishes. They may be of two kinds—(*a*) for those who are definitely attached to the Church, (*b*) for all and sundry. The second sort may seem to be of less direct spiritual value, and they need not necessarily be in direct connection with the parish church ; but there will be serious loss if " the Church " takes no interest in them (*e.g.*, Y.M.C.A.).

There is a great future for clubs where men and girls can meet together naturally under healthy conditions.

G. Special Classes of Parishioners.

(1) *Men.*—Branch of C.E.M.S. (The Church House, Westminster, S.W.1).

(2) *Women.*—Branch of Mothers' Union (Church House, Westminster, S.W.1).

Women's Help Society (Church House, Westminster, S.W.1).

Mothers' Meeting, or Women's Fellowship.

(3) *Lads.*—Church Lads' Brigade and Church Scouts (Aldwych House, Catherine Street, W.C.2).

Boy Scouts (Headquarters, 18 Henrietta St., W.C.2).

Boys' Brigade (Paternoster House, E.C.4).

As it is probable that all boys will in future be drafted into cadet corps, it is important that our Church boys should be enlisted in a recognised cadet corps, which is religious in its aim. C.L.B. is so recognised.

(4) *Girls.*—Girls' Friendly Society (Headquarters, G.F.S. Central Office, 39 Victoria Street, S.W.1).

Girl Guides (Headquarters, 116 Victoria St., S.W.1).

Church Nursing and Ambulance Brigade (Headquarters, Queen Street, Marble Arch, W.2).

H. Finance.—The finance of the parish will probably be managed by the Parish Council. Sometimes the free-will-offering association is separately organised.

In town parishes it is usually desirable to separate *poor relief* as far as possible from the ordinary work of the parish. Sometimes a poor relief committee with representatives of the wage-earners is useful.

On the whole subject of relief, see C. F. Rogers' "Charitable Relief" (Longmans).

II. Ruridecanal.

A. Central.

(1) *The Ruridecanal Chapter.*

(2) *The Ruridecanal Conference.*

There will often be permanent committees dealing with education, social service, etc.

B. Churches of the Deanery.

(1) *Association of Lay Readers.*—There is usually a diocesan organisation, but a deanery or group of deaneries can often arrange classes, lectures, etc.

(2) In a town of considerable size it may be good to arrange *special services* in a central church, *e.g.*, midday services in Lent, or services for different classes of people—medical profession, artists, railwaymen, sailors, telegraph messengers, etc., etc.

C. Evangelistic and Pastoral.

(1) *Care of Institutions.*

(*a*) Workhouse (where the Board of Guardians do not appoint a chaplain).

(*b*) Hospitals and infirmaries.

(*c*) Hospitals for infectious diseases: it is obviously unfair that the whole responsibility should rest on the parish in which such a hospital happens to be placed. It is a scandal if such hospitals do not receive spiritual care.

(2) *A Ruridecanal Board of Missions* (closely connected with the Diocesan Board) will be an invaluable stimulus to missionary work.

D. Educational.

(1) *Association of Church Day Schools*, linked up with the Diocesan Association. The Act of 1918 may probably render concerted action (*e.g.*, for establishing upper standard schools) necessary.

(2) *Association of Day School Teachers.*—*E.g.*, branch of St. Peter's Guild (Secretary, Rev. W. C. Piercy, St. Nicholas Cole Abbey Rectory, Lambeth Hill, E.C.4), or Guild of Good Shepherd (Secretary, Sister Mary Beatrice, St. Mary's Home, Wantage).

(3) Lectures and Classes for *intending teachers.* Also, where possible, lectures for teachers.

(4) *Sunday School Teachers' Association.*

E. Social and Moral.

(1) *Vigilance Association.*

(2) *Rescue and Preventive Association* (generally worked on Diocesan lines).

(3) Branch of *Christian Social Union* (Secretary, L. V. Lester Garland, 26 Norfolk Square, W.2).

Social Service Committee, for promotion of better housing, infant welfare, and other branches of social reform.

F. Social and Recreational.—Parishes may often with advantage combine for organisation of clubs, etc.

G. Special Classes.

(1) Parochial organisations often may be linked together, *e.g.*, Federation of C.E.M.S., Battalion of C.L.B., including parochial companies, etc.

(2) Care of blind.

(3) Care of deaf and dumb.

In many of these agencies it is obviously desirable (even necessary) that we should combine with all Christian people who are ready to work with us. This applies specially to witness on behalf of purity and temperance, to social welfare work, and to a good deal of educational work.

Moreover, experience has proved the good results of united evangelistic effort, *e.g.*, services in a public hall or in the open air.

CHAPTER XIII

THE CHURCH AND THE SOCIAL MOVEMENT

AT this stage in our inquiry the question might well be asked—How has the experience of the past five years modified our conception of pastoral life and work? There are certainly new elements in the position. The experience of many of the chaplains at the front, our own observation of new tendencies (for good far more than for evil) among our people at home, our more careful diagnosis of our own failures, and above all the sense of a tremendous responsibility laid on the Church by the splendid hopes and aspirations of a new time, are bound to have a far-reaching effect on our own ideals of priestly ministry. Doubtless there are principles of pastoral life which are constant. The message of God's love in Jesus Christ is the same as ever : the sacraments of His grace are unchanged ; still God is to be worshipped and His teaching made known ; still the priest must labour faithfully for the conversion of individual souls ; now as always we must plead for the recognition of Christ's presence in home and in school. But we have tried to see many of these things in a new light; to give clearer expression to our aim, and to remember that the Church will be strong in so far as it forgets its own apparent interests in its witness for the kingdom of God, while it exhibits the warm and loving fellowship of a great brotherhood. We have been led to recognise that real service is a stronger motive than self-interest, and that the comfort which we are privileged to minister to the souls of men is no narcotic, but an inspiration for new venture, bringing them God's peace in order that they may fight better in God's war.

I. There is another word to be added. If the Church is indeed the " light of the world," it must illuminate great movements of the time, which, by whatever human imperfection they may be hindered, are the result of aspirations essentially Christian. The Church ought to be able to give to these aspirations their best and highest expression, and to supply the divine power without which the true goal can never be attained. The whole body of the Church must do its part, but its officers ought to lead. Nothing could be more miserable than that the priests of the Church should be so immersed in petty parochial administration, or so preoccupied with details of ecclesiastical tradition, that they stand severely aloof from movements which are changing the whole face of the country. It is said—I know not with what truth— that after the war of 1870, the Church in France was unable to do anything more than to offer certain new devotions to the faithful; it knew not the day of its visitation, and lost its God-given opportunity. We believe that it is finding and using its opportunity to-day. God help us to do the same.

There are movements indeed within the Church itself which claim our active interest. There are, for example, two great causes which call for the enthusiastic devotion of all Christians, and about which, even after all our bitter experiences, some so-called churchmen care nothing at all, namely, the spread of the Gospel throughout all the world, and the reunion of Christendom : a priest is no true priest if he does not pray and work for these two glorious ends ; for they embody most directly and immediately the purpose which our Lord set before us—" Seek ye first the kingdom of God and His righteousness."

II. But I have in my mind other movements which, having for their aim the establishment of righteousness, brotherhood, and peace among all nations and within the nation itself, are equally Christian in their essence, because they tend towards the establishment of the sovereignty of God over the common life of men. Though they are not in the narrower sense of the word "ecclesiastical," it will be disastrous indeed if the Church holds aloof from them.

Twenty-four years ago Bishop Westcott delivered his famous charge, "The Incarnation a Revelation of Human Duties." He contended that when He took on Him our human nature, God gave us the assurance that nothing human is alien to Him, and that He claims every part of our life for His own; seeing that all humanity is summed up in the incarnate Word of God, the solidarity of our race is a fact which no Christian can doubt, and therefore each unit in human society must be free to develop its own life to perfection in order that it may make its proper contribution to the good of the whole. He applied these principles to the two great movements of international amity and of social justice, which he taught us to regard as subjects not merely for political adjustment, but for the practical application of the Christian creed.

He declared his belief that the twentieth century would witness the bringing in of a better order of social fellowship, but he could not have foreseen through what terrible experiences we should travel towards that goal. At the present time there is not one thoughtful person among the allied peoples who does not see that the hope for the future rests on a league of fellowship among the nations which shall secure something far better than the peace of mere inaction. So long indeed as there is still a nation which holds the hateful doctrine that the nation is above God, and that it may use any means for the establishment of its own world power, force must conquer force until such a nation is ready to accept right, in the place of might, as the arbiter of national destinies. But the aim is clear—that each nation, great or small, shall be free to live its own life and develop its own gifts, spiritual and material, for the good of all : and that all the nations should be united in a league to secure the establishment of a law of public right throughout the world. No one pretends that the lines of national liberty can be readily and quickly drawn, or that a league of nations is an ideal easy of attainment ; but that it is a Christian ideal, the direct result of a belief in the Incarnation, no well-instructed Christian can doubt : and we are sure that only through the application of Christian principles, by the frank acceptance of the kingdom of God as the ultimate aim, and by trust in the power of God as the one sufficient motive power, can the ideal be translated into action.

III. Of the kindred movement within the nation itself, arising out of the aspiration after a better social order to be based on justice and fellowship among men, I shall speak at greater length, because it bears more closely on the daily life and witness of a parish priest. Let us first consider what are the Christian principles on which any sound plan of social reform must be based.

We might indeed approach the subject from the side of Christian expediency. The outward circumstances of men's lives have a real influence on their moral and spiritual growth. This point is well put in the Interim Report of the Committee on Adult Education (issued September 1918), presided over by the Master of Balliol. The Report argues that there is need for such a reconstruction of conditions of daily life and work as will afford men and women greater opportunities for satisfying that craving for education in its widest sense which is a permanent human need —the desire " for knowledge, for self-expression, for the satisfaction of intellectual, æsthetic, and spiritual needs, and a fuller life."

The proposals urged by the committee are as follows :—

" A maximum legal working day of eight hours, with strict regulation of overtime and night work.

Effective measures to ensure reasonable security of livelihood by guarding against and mitigating the effects of unemployment.

Reasonable holidays with pay for wage-earners.

A comprehensive scheme of housing reform, in the carrying out of which women should have an effective voice.

Reconstruction in the conditions of rural life ; a public hall for every village."

Excessive and irregular hours of work are specially pointed to by the committee as tending to unfit the worker for taking advantage of educational opportunities.

All that is said of the cramping and chilling effect of bad industrial conditions on educational progress is also true of the obstacles which they offer to a full spiritual life. It is doubtless a stupid fallacy to imagine that good environment is the one thing needed for good Christian character : some of the worst people whom any of us have known have lived all their lives in excellent surroundings, and some of the best have been among the poorest. But any parish priest who has kept his eyes open can witness to the intolerable hindrances to a Christian life which beset the workers in many parts of our industrial system. It is not material poverty in itself which is the difficulty, although the degrading destitution of a slum differs *toto caelo* from the poverty of the fishermen of Galilee. The trouble arises from the poverty of opportunity, the strain of monotonous occupations, the moral and physical unhealthiness of overcrowded dwellings. We are fools and blind if we allow these evils to continue without effective protest.

We ought, however, to approach the subject from a higher ground than that of expediency. We must look at the whole question in the light of the witness and teaching of our Lord. It will only be possible to touch very briefly on a very great subject.

(1) We have already considered that the "taking of manhood into God" at the Incarnation implies the claim of God over every part of our human life. The Son of God came that we may have life, and may have it abundantly. All humanity is "summed up"[1] in the Son of Man, and finds unity and fellowship in Him.

(2) Each child of God is of infinite and equal value in His sight. Therefore it must always be wrong to use any human being for less than a human purpose, whether it be pleasure, or lust, or profit. A man cannot be a mere instrument of production. Personal life is the end, property at its best only a means.

(3) The belief in the infinite value of each individual, with the claim for individual liberty which follows upon it, needs to be balanced by the belief in the brotherhood of all men. We are all children of the one Father; we are "all one man in Christ Jesus."[2]

Therefore mutual service is the rule of our life, after the example of Him who came among us as "He that serveth."[3] Industry should be regarded as a service for the common good, not as a mere means of personal profit.

(4) If we are brethren, it follows that we are responsible one for another. Whatever advantages anyone possesses he holds in trust for all. Because we must give account of our time, idleness is a sin

[1] Eph. i. 10.   [2] Gal. iii. 28.   [3] St. Luke xxii. 27.

10

whether in rich or poor. Because we must give account of our money, we have to take careful heed to our means of acquiring it, and our manner of spending it. The sin of Dives lay not in his possession of much wealth, but in the fact that, having a great responsibility, he did nothing.

This is, after all, a series of truisms : yet if members of the Christian Church had acted on these truisms, human society would have been revolutionised from top to bottom. There have been times when Christians acted on these principles, when they really valued human personality above wealth, and lived as brethren. We cannot honestly say that since the industrial revolution in the beginning of the nineteenth century the witness of the Christian Church has shown much force and courage. There have been great prophets like Maurice, Kingsley, Westcott, and Holland ;[1] there have (it is needless to say) been a multitude of honest men in all classes who have loved God and their neighbours and have done their best under difficult conditions. But we cannot say that the mass of Christians have even attempted to apply their Christianity to social and industrial life. The worst of it is that even now there are people who say that it is " unspiritual " to claim God's sovereignty over daily business, and are there not a few priests who think in their heart of hearts that the world is quite a good place as it is, and that if there are social evils they do not require very drastic remedies ?

How are we to do our duty better ? Certainly we should not pretend to be economic experts, or proclaim some one political or social theory as the panacea of all ills. Still less can we consent to be mere party politicians. But we must be in earnest about the matter, and our repentance for past blindness or inactivity will be none the less real because

[1] The Lambeth Conference of Bishops in 1888, 1897, 1908 gave a strong lead with regard to the Church's duty in social questions. It was very poorly followed.

we have a strong hope for the future. There are many men and women among us now who are seeing a new vision, and who are resolved that, after the gigantic waste of war, at least the new opportunity shall not be wasted, and the growing spirit of willing service for the common good shall not be lost; that the war of classes shall not begin afresh, and that the old futilities of party recrimination shall not revive.

The great and crying need is a new spirit—the Christ spirit of love, and liberty, and brotherhood. But lest this chapter should be accused of vagueness, let me venture to suggest some items in a policy of social reconstruction; of course there is nothing original in them.

(1) Men and women must count as persons and not as mere "hands." They must have some active part in the control of the industry to which their lives are given.

(2) There must be a "living wage" for all; reasonable leisure; and protection against the accident of unemployment.

(3) So long as the present organisation of industry lasts, there is need for the freest conference between employers and workmen on the lines of the *Whitley Report*. But, as Bishop Westcott said, "Wage-labour, though it appears to be an inevitable step in the evolution of society, is as little fitted to represent finally or adequately the connection of man with man in the production of wealth as, at earlier times, slavery and serfdom."

(4) The surplus profits of production ought to belong to the community rather than to the capitalist.

(5) Men must have homes, not hovels to live in; and our towns must be something better than a mean wilderness of dirty streets. There must also be a complete regeneration of rural life.

(6) There must be a real education for the children,

an education which aims at making them, not better instruments of production, but men and women capable of rendering a full and happy service to the community.

Even so mild an instalment of reforms will be opposed by two different advocates of force. The Prussianist, who still exists in England, talks of "keeping the working man in his proper place"; he desires to perpetuate military methods in industrial organisation, not for the sake of the public safety and the common good, but for the security of the money interests of his own class. The Bolshevist desires to perpetuate class warfare in order that he may bring about a social revolution; he continually repeats that "class warfare is a fact," by which he really means that he intends class warfare to go on until every class but one (his own) is abolished. The Christian must be as militant as Prussian or Bolshevist, but his warfare is to be waged against selfishness and injustice, in himself first, and then wherever he finds them in the world around.

Indeed the weapons of Christian warfare will be sorely needed if the battle of the better social order is to be won. We thank God that the nation is full of noble ideals, but there will be need for great self-sacrifice and courage if the *vis inertiae* of human selfishness and the craftiness of the mammon worshipper are to be overcome. Here indeed is a warfare in which all Christian men, and some men of good will who do not call themselves Christians, must act as one. Without the power of the Divine Leader we shall certainly fail. With Him we can remove mountains.

IV. It may be asked—In what way can parish priests give practical help to the cause of social progress?

First it is to be remembered that this is a matter for the whole Church. Our part in the movement may be to lead, but often enough we shall gladly follow the lead of a layman better qualified than ourselves.

(1) We can practise and promote the study of social and industrial questions. A branch of the Christian Social Union will be a help towards this end.[1]

(2) We ought, as priests, to understand and sympathise with the difficulties of all parties. When all classes in the community are fully represented, as they ought to be, in the priesthood, our independence of class prejudice will be more clearly established than it is to-day. But even now we should try to be men who are apart from all "class" feeling, and no men have a better chance of meeting all classes on a footing of equality. If a dispute is unfortunately going on we shall not rush to a conclusion as to the merits of the case. It is only on very rare occasions that we shall be of any service as mediators. There have been times when a priest who has established his position in the confidence of his people, and is known and trusted for his wisdom, and fairness, and sympathy, has been asked to mediate ; but he

---

[1] The present officers of the C.S.U. are :—

President : The Right Rev. the Lord Bishop of Lichfield.
Vice-Presidents : The Right Rev. the Lord Bishop of Winchester. The Right Rev. the Lord Bishop of Liverpool. The Rev. John Carter.
General Secretary and *Acting Hon. Treasurer :* L. V. Lester-Garland, 26 Norfolk Square, W.2.

The C.S.U. consists of members of the Church of England, or of any body in full communion with her, who have the following objects at heart :—

(1) To claim for the Christian law the ultimate authority to rule social practice.

(2) To study in common how to apply the moral truths and principles of Christianity to the social and economic difficulties of the present time.

(3) To present Christ in practical life as the living Master and King, the enemy of wrong and selfishness, the power of righteousness and love.

is always the last man to be intrusive or to advertise himself.

(3) It is most important that men who apply their Christianity to political and social life, and who are above the suspicion of having any axe to grind, should be ready to serve on public bodies. This applies chiefly to our best laymen. But clergy may do most useful work on local Education Authorities and Boards of Guardians.

(4) The clergy and their workers are in possession of a great store of knowledge with regard to the life of the people and their real needs. It is unfortunate that this knowledge is seldom available for purposes of social legislation and administration. In the work of relieving poverty, the clergy have often (not always) made use of accurate knowledge, and acted on wise principles. Why is it that we have been so far less effective in using our knowledge for the prevention of poverty? Again, in matters of social reform, such as the promotion of a good housing policy, the clergy and their helpers might render invaluable service in providing accurate information and stimulating public opinion.

(5) From time to time the clergy have the opportunity of actively promoting measures for the welfare of their people. For example—some clergy have rendered excellent service in helping women workers to organise themselves for protection against sweating: there are country clergy who have promoted co-operative enterprise among the farmers; other instances would not be difficult to find.

(6) None of these activities are "secular." But a priest in the Church of God will never forget to lead his people in intercession for the coming of the kingdom of God, in our social life; in other words, for the recognition of Jesus Christ as our living Master and King, whose law must have the ultimate authority to rule all social practice.

CHAPTER XIV

STUDY

THE bare outline which this book has given of the life and duty of a priest, with the opportunities which this "Day of the Lord" has presented to us, and the demands which it makes upon us, may have brought home to our consciences a sense of our unworthiness for so tremendous a responsibility, and our insufficiency for so magnificent a work. We need to give our minds to study, and our wills to discipline, and above all, with the consciousness that we can do nothing without the renewing power of the Holy Spirit, to lay our hearts open to His inspiration by the reality of our devotional life.

At our ordination we promised to "be diligent in prayers, and in reading of the Holy Scriptures, and in such studies as help to the knowledge of the same, laying aside the study of the world and of the flesh." That is to say, we solemnly promised to be life-long students.

We shall never be good teachers unless we keep the springs of our knowledge constantly fresh, and now that education is becoming more widely diffused, and happily more purposeful and effective, we shall be justly despised if we do not even try to keep abreast with the knowledge and intelligence of our people. Many of them, as we have seen, are lamentably ignorant of the Christian religion : but if it is a mistake to overrate their knowledge, it is a worse error to underrate their intelligence. This, however, is not the only reason why we ought to be students. Each of us must constantly rededicate himself as a sacrifice to God. He needs our devotion first of all, and He calls on us for active work, but our sacrifice is miserably incomplete if we do not dedicate our intellects to Him. Our very activity will be in danger of becoming a worthless offering, if there is no knowledge and very little thought at the back of it. We shall do well to remember St. Bernard's dictum, " Sunt qui scire volunt ut sciant, et turpis curiositas est ; et sunt qui scire volunt ut sciantur ipsi, et turpis vanitas est ; et sunt qui scire volunt ut scientiam suam vendant, et turpis quaestus est ; et sunt quoque qui scire volunt ut aedificent, et caritas est." St. Bernard will have no self-seeking in our pursuit of knowledge, but no one knew better than he that knowledge is a first necessity for " building up " Christian life and character. Bishop Westcott meant the same thing when he gave as his maxim for students, " Study liberally, think seriously, serve gladly."

I. **The Scope of our Study.**—The main subject of our study must be theology, by which we mean the intellectual exposition of Christian verity. The court of appeal to which all theology must be referred is the Bible, and therefore the question in the Ordinal places Holy Scripture first among our studies : but it goes on to speak of " such studies as help to the knowledge of the same," and these cover a very large field. " All things," said our Lord, " that the Father hath are Mine," [1] and among the " all things " must certainly be included the world of nature which God created and upholds, and the life of man who is made in the image of God, and whose manhood was taken into God at the Incarnation. The study of science, history, and literature may indeed be a study of the worldly world if God is left out of it, but it may

---

[1] St. John xvi. 15.

be so pursued as to give us a fuller and deeper knowledge of God's wisdom and loving providence.

It is clearly impossible for every parish priest to be an accomplished scientist or historian. No one expects it of us. But we ought to have that good general education which enables us to gain the right attitude of mind towards all the best activities of human thought. We should understand what is meant by scientific method, some knowledge of philosophy will be of immense service as a groundwork for our theology (how many of the best divines have been Platonists!), and if a man is specially interested in any subject, whether scientific or literary, apart from the study of theology, by all means let him continue to cultivate it. The really important matter is that we should have a close enough touch with the subjects in which men are interested, to enable us to sympathise with them and to interpret God's revelation to them in terms of current thought and in language which they can understand. If we can only express our theology in text-book language, as though it were a lesson we had learned by rote, it will seem to them to be unreal and unrelated to life as they know it.

II. **Our Liberty as Students.**—Nevertheless, sacred learning is our principal subject of study. For most clergy the important thing is that they should know their Bible thoroughly well and be constantly increasing their knowledge of doctrine and history, as they bear on the problems of life. Natural modesty will save a man from fancying himself a learned critic when he does not know the A.B.C. of scholarship ; but while it is true that comparatively few priests have the gifts which will enable them to be really profound scholars, capable of working out their own research, it will be a bad day for the Church if it lacks learned and scholarly theologians among its clergy.

Here, however, we are met with a difficulty. " A

scholar," it is argued, "must be free to follow his researches without reserve, and must honestly accept the conclusions to which he is led. But as an accredited teacher of the Church a priest must be faithful to the Church's creeds. How then can a priest be an honest scholar if he has formed his conclusions before he begins his research?" We answer at once that every man is bound to accept what he believes to be the truth; if (which God forbid should happen) a priest arrives, as a result of his study, at the denial of what the Church holds to be true, we cannot ask him to be false to his own convictions; only we shall be sure that he will see the impossibility of retaining his position as a teacher in the Church whose creed he denies. In no case will the Church condemn him for following his convictions; it can only say, "Such and such is the revelation committed to the Church; you cannot be one of our teachers if you deny what the Church affirms."

But, after all, is it right that a priest of the Church should enter on a course of study with absolutely free and unfettered judgment? Assuredly *yes*, for we are never afraid of truth; moreover (to take a lower ground), scholarship must be met by scholarship, and the negative critics have not hitherto had the monopoly of scholarly learning and critical acumen. It may, however, be doubted whether anyone is capable of divesting his mind of all presuppositions. The negative critic can seldom rid himself of the assumption that miracles never happen. The Christian scholar starts with the presupposition that it is "natural" for God to enter into fellowship with men; and his experience of the uniqueness of Jesus Christ is part of himself; he knows Whom he has believed; moreover, the experience of the saints in all the ages (which is another name for the authority of the Church) is, to his way of thinking, not a negligible factor in the inquiry.

Nevertheless, the " Christ of experience " can only be severed from the " Christ of history " at the cost of reducing the Christian religion to an uncertain system of vague emotion : and we who believe that Jesus of Nazareth is the incarnate God, must be prepared to examine with the utmost care the documentary and other evidence on which we base our historical knowledge of His presence, His words, and His actions in this world. We cannot refuse, and we have no cause to fear, the closest and most scientific criticism of the New Testament as well as the Old Testament books. We do not pretend that we can rid our minds of all presuppositions—no students, certainly not the negative critics, have succeeded in doing so—but we try to approach the question with an open mind, and many of us, as the result of honest investigation, have come to a stronger conviction than ever that it is those who deny the historicity of the miraculous element in the Gospel history, not those who affirm it, who are doing violence to the facts. Historical study only serves to reinforce the belief of our innermost experience in the uniqueness of Jesus Christ.[1]

[1] The object of this section is simply to vindicate the liberty of the clergy to do their work thoroughly as scholars, and at the same time to affirm the obvious fact that the accredited teachers of the Church must teach what the Church holds to be truth. It is not within the compass of this book to deal with current controversies on the creeds. I accept *ex animo* the resolution passed by the Upper House of Canterbury Convocation on 30th April 1914 :—" Inasmuch as there is reason to believe that the minds of many members of the Church of England are perplexed and disquieted at the present time in regard to certain questions of faith and Church order, the bishops of the Upper House of the Province of Canterbury feel it to be their duty to put forth the following resolutions : (1) We call attention to the resolution which was passed in this House on 10th May 1905, as follows : 'That this House is resolved to maintain unimpaired the Catholic faith in the holy Trinity, and the Incarnation as contained in the Apostles' and Nicene Creeds, and in the Quicunque vult, and regards the faith presented, both in state-

III. **Some Principles of Theological Study.**—
There are many clergy to whom this plea for liberty
of scholarship will not in the least appeal. It is true
enough that comparatively few priests have the
necessary equipment for independent study; if this
be so, at least they ought to sympathise with the
scholar, and to avoid the folly of condemning a
"criticism" which they do not understand; indeed,
one may go further and plead that many of them
ought to learn something of the work of the best
scholars and historians, for the Church has never
been obscurantist in its outlook, and the priests of
the Church can never be despisers of knowledge.

But this chapter will perhaps serve its purpose
best if it sets forth some quite general principles of
theological study, and I will put them in the form
of some counsels addressed to the younger clergy.

(1) Find the *right central point* for all your reading.

ments of doctrine and in statements of fact, as the necessary
basis on which the teaching of the Church reposes.' We
further desire to direct attention afresh to the following
resolution which was unanimously agreed to by the bishops of
the Anglican communion attending the Lambeth Conference of
1906 : 'This conference, in view of the tendencies widely
shown in the writings of the present day, hereby places on
record its conviction that the historical facts stated in the
creeds are an essential part of the faith of the Church.' (2)
These resolutions we desire solemnly to reaffirm, and in accordance therewith to express our deliberate judgment that the
denial of any of the historical facts stated in the creeds goes
beyond the limits of legitimate interpretation, and gravely
imperils the sincerity of profession which is plainly incumbent
upon the ministers of the word and sacraments. At the same
time, recognising that our generation is called to face new
problems raised by historical criticism, we are anxious not to
lay unnecessary burdens on consciences nor unduly to limit
freedom of thought and inquiry, whether among clergy or
among laity. We desire, therefore, to lay stress on the need of
considerateness in dealing with that which is tentative and
provisional in the thought and work of earnest and reverent
students."

There is a tendency, perhaps encouraged by some of our examinations, to regard the subjects of theological study as a series of disconnected items—the Bible, the Prayer Book, Church History, the Thirty-Nine Articles, etc. In reality the study of the divine revelation is one connected whole, and the centre of it is the Incarnation of the Son of God. The Old Testament is the record of how in times past, "by many parts and in many fashions, God spake unto the fathers by the prophets," treating His people as the sacred school of training for the time when He should speak to men through His Son. The New Testament gives us the gospel of the incarnation, showing us how the Word became flesh and dwelt among us, full of grace and truth, revealing to us the Father, redeeming us for His service, pouring upon us the gifts of His Spirit, uniting us in His family.

Christian doctrine is simply a development of the belief in the incarnation. It deals with the subject of our Lord's person, of His revelation of the nature of God and the destiny of man, and of His saving and sanctifying work. In the liturgies of the Church we can illustrate the *lex credendi* by the *lex orandi*, both of which are meaningless apart from the incarnate Son of God.

Moral theology is not only an exposition of the eternal principles of divine righteousness and love which find their full expression in the teaching of our Lord : it is also a development of that new conception of man's relationship to God and to his fellows which is inherent in the person of the Son of God, who is also Son of Man. A Christian ethic of social and international relationships is implied in St. Paul's great saying, " There is neither Jew nor Greek, there is neither bond nor free, there is neither male nor female : for ye are all one man in Christ Jesus." [1]

[1] Gal. iii. 28.

Church history is the record of the work which, in spite of human follies and sins, the ever-present Lord has continued to accomplish for the salvation of men. Its first chapter is the Acts of the Apostles, the most recent chapter is the record of the missionary work of these latest days; the conclusion will not be reached till He hath put all things under His feet.

The comparative study of religions teaches us not to despise the truths which "the light who lighteneth every man coming into the world" has made known to those who in dark places have been feeling after God, while it demonstrates to us that the best thoughts of these other religions are as the twinkling of stars compared with the full sunshine of the truth, beauty, and goodness revealed in Jesus Christ.

(2) While our first need is to consider how the subject which we are studying takes its place in the closely related scheme of theology, our second principle is to *read our subject thoroughly*, working all round it, and not approaching it merely from one view-point. We need not be afraid of books written by authors not of our own communion : "they shall go in and out and find pasture." But we shall above all try always to keep on hand some really great book by one of our own divines, such a book as Butler's "Analogy," or Hort's "The Way, the Truth, and the Life," or Westcott's "Gospel of Life," or Moberly's "Atonement and Personality," or one of Dean Church's volumes. Let us beware of controversial treatises, written by some partizan, and dealing chiefly with negations : it is always worth while at least to try to understand the point of view of those whose theology does not appeal to us, and I believe that the best minds are always desirous of finding an Eirenicon which may unite the largest possible number of Christian believers on a comprehensive basis of positive belief.

(3) Much of our reading must be done in solitude. But there ought in every deanery to be opportunity for "iron to sharpen iron" by some plan of *associated study*; in each deanery there should be a study secretary who keeps the clergy in touch with the Central Society of Sacred Study, organising lectures and study circles, and arranging (wherever possible) library facilities for the clergy.

(4) It is hardly necessary to say that reasonable time must be reserved for study. Most clergy can keep at least a considerable part of their mornings free for reading, apart from the time spent in preparing sermons or addresses.

(5) Our study will avail nothing without the guidance of the Holy Spirit. We can claim our Lord's promise, "He shall guide you into all truth." Surely He expects us to put forth our very best powers, to "study liberally and think seriously"; but He will illuminate our natural intelligence with His supernatural wisdom, and lead us along the two roads of contemplation and active service to that knowledge of God which is Life Eternal.

CHAPTER XV

SELF-DISCIPLINE

No army can exist without discipline. Order is heaven's first law, and if the Church is the army of the kingdom of heaven, there must be order within its ranks; if the clergy are to be leaders in the spiritual war, they must be disciplined men. But this discipline must be self-imposed, for there is no class of men in the community who are so free as the clergy to live their lives in their own way. There is indeed the authority of the bishop, to whom priests and deacons promise "canonical obedience," but every bishop desires to rule his diocese as a father rather than as a despot, and to appeal to the consciences of his clergy rather than to apply any form of coercion. There are also clear directions laid down in the Prayer Book which bishops and priests alike are bound to obey; but again it depends on a man's own conscience whether, for example, he obeys the rule of saying morning and evening prayer, or whether he makes excuses for disregarding it.

For a man of God the rule of conscience ought to be the strongest rule in the world, and the absence of outward authority with the sanction of force to back it up is compatible with the most complete discipline—such discipline as that of the angelic armies of heaven, whose motto is "God's will is our law." But this means that we must deal strictly with ourselves: "tantum proficies quantum tibi ipsi vim intuleris." For those who are filled with a burning love for God, rules may be unnecessary, but for most of us "the liberty of the glory of the sons of God" can only be won by hard self-discipline.

In considering how and where this discipline must be applied, I shall follow very simple and obvious lines. We will deal with the necessity of self-discipline with regard to the use of our time, the care of money, the restraint of temper, and the control of our desires and passions.

I. Our Time.—A priest has more liberty in the regulation of his time than can be found in any other profession or employment. The artisan "loses a quarter" if he does not arrive at the works at 6 A.M. The clerk has to keep regular hours. The medical man and the lawyer have some latitude as to the arrangement of their time, but if they are casual and irregular their practice will be wrecked and their income will disappear. The priest alone has absolute freedom to spend his time as he thinks well; the result is that he may be either the busiest man in his parish, or he may be the laziest. Hence arises the strange fact that some good people regard the clergy as overworked, while others envy them the "softness" of their job. I have no doubt Mr. Walter Carey is right when he says that "the hundred hardest worked men in England are clergy; and the hundred vilest slackers are clergy." [1] The first hundred possess a conscience and discipline themselves; the second hundred go as they please and let things slide; they may have started out with excellent intentions, but their utter lack of method and their objection to discipline have resulted in complacent satisfaction with the performance of a few "duties," and in a condition of almost vegetable inertia.

It is obvious that if we are to spend our time well, we must plan out a self-imposed rule in the use of it. We shall have a regular time for rising in the morning

[1] Rev. W. J. Carey, "My Priesthood" (Longmans), p. 37.

11

I would begin with a few pagan virtues ; we will come to your phraseology by and by."

There can be no doubt that the poverty of many of the clergy causes the gravest difficulty. Some day, let us hope the day may be soon, we shall (please God) so reform our finance that all clergy shall be paid a living wage. But at present many priests have a hard struggle to keep out of debt. Yet the effort must be made, for it is ruinous to a man's influence if he is known to owe money right and left among his parishioners. Another danger arises from the various accounts which the parish priest may be expected to keep—though he will be wise if he leaves parish funds in the hands of the laity. He should have separate accounts at the bank for parochial and personal funds, and separate cash boxes for the petty cash. Such details seem trivial, but the line between muddle and dishonesty is not always very easily drawn. A priest ought to be a good business man if that somewhat doubtful term means accuracy and care in money matters, and a mind which combines boldness of venture with a careful husbanding of resources.

III. **Restraint of Temper.** — Bishop Lonsdale might have added to his list of " Pagan virtues," " Can he keep his temper ? " Anger is by no means always a sin. Some of us ought to be more capable of it than we are. But bad temper rising out of merely personal causes, and leading to quarrels and divisions, may be a sin of a peculiarly scandalous sort. Pride is usually at the root of it. A man is determined to have his own way, or has an exalted idea of his own dignity. Possibly he is spoilt by the deference shown to him by his own adherents, and is resentful because other people do not pay him proper respect. A sense of humour is a good antidote against this kind of folly and it is well for us to remember that our influence may depend more than we know on our courtesy and kindliness of temper in all sorts of places and on all occasions.

One source of irritation is perhaps worthy of mention. It is trying when the praises of a predecessor are constantly dinned into our ears. There are few better tests of Christian temper, and just discrimination, than is shown in appreciation of a predecessor ; and there is no greater example of folly than a determination to make as many alterations as possible in the customs and methods which he has left behind him, unless it be the stupidity of perpetually singing the praises of one's own former parish.

IV. **Our Desires and Passions.**—We turn to the most serious region for the exercise of self-discipline. If we are inclined to forget that we are men, subject to a man's passions and desires, we may be sure that the devil will not forget it. From time to time we hear of some terrible priestly downfall which reminds us of hidden fires which few of us have wholly subdued, and of a possible encounter with gross temptations against which there is no safeguard except strong self-discipline and constant reliance on the all-sufficient grace of God. If St. Paul found it necessary to buffet his body and bring it into subjection, it is not likely that we shall be superior to the need of discipline.

The danger of drunkenness may be remote, but one may be sure that the drunkard priests—who, alas ! do exist—slipped into their miserable state by imperceptible degrees. My own belief is that total abstinence from alcohol is desirable for the great majority of clergy, not, of course, because alcohol is an evil thing in itself, nor merely because a total abstainer has immense advantages in tackling the sin of intemperance, but because it is a sound piece of self-discipline and cuts off a possible occasion of falling.

CHAPTER XVI

THE DEVOTIONAL LIFE OF THE PRIEST [1]

THE supreme need of the priest is that he should keep in close contact with our Lord. Whether we consider the greatness and the difficulties of our calling, or the failures in our own personal characters and the temptations which beset us, as men and as priests, it is evident that we must rely on a power not our own. "When I am weak," exclaims St. Paul, "then I am strong," [2] that is to say, "When I have learnt my own powerlessness, then I can throw myself with absolute confidence on the infinite power of God." If we could at all times realise the inexhaustible wealth of the resources of God, which are revealed in Jesus Christ and ministered to us through His eternal Spirit, we should go about our work with glad serenity and imperturbable trust, fighting the good fight with peace in our hearts, and reflecting in quiet but intensely active service the redemptive love of the Good Shepherd.

But this sure hold on the divine resources, this personal touch with our Lord Himself, depends on the reality of our devotional life,—on our communions, our prayers, our meditation on the revelation of the truth as it is in Jesus.

What point of departure shall we take? In con-

[1] With regard to this subject, see Dr. A. W. Robinson, "Personal Life of the Clergy" (Longmans).

[2] 2 Cor. xii. 10.

sidering our aim we looked to that aim which our Lord made His own: in treating of priesthood we set before ourselves the one High Priest; all our ministry of truth and grace, of word and sacrament, is His ministry. Shall we not then look to Him as the example and the source of that life of devotion on which all else must depend? It is sacred ground to tread. There are depths in the inner life of our blessed Lord which we can never fathom. Yet we cannot be content with any but the highest standard, and in the Gospels the veil is at times withdrawn which hides the sanctuary of the Lord's life of perfect communion with the Father, and we may, for example, reverently meditate on the great priestly intercession recorded in St. John's Gospel,[1] and learn from it something of the secret of that intercession which He never ceases to offer on our behalf.

(1) *Penitence.*—There is indeed one side of our devotion, the life of penitence, in which it seems at first sight that the disciple cannot be as his Master. He was sinless, we are sinful, and our whole life must be a school time of repentance. We have already[2] reminded ourselves that penitence, which is the first condition of peace and joy, bears its best fruit when we are sure of God's forgiveness. The greatest saints are always the truest penitents, and the man who is nearest to God declares, without any sort of unreality, that he is the chief of sinners. Of course, he is not always thinking about his sins, but he thinks a great deal about the love of God, who has forgiven him so much, and the consciousness of that love impels him to venture all in the great service to which God calls him.

Yet it may truly be affirmed that even here our Lord leads the way. Dr. Moberly[3] has taught us that there is a true sense in which our Lord's offering on the Cross was the offering of a perfect repentance.

---

[1] St. John xvii. [2] Chapter IX.
[3] Moberly's (R. C.) "Atonement and Personality" (J. Murray).

"Mysteriously the whole world's sin, His, and not His, is blended in." Himself sinless, He identifies Himself so perfectly and absolutely with His brethren that He offers a true repentance on their behalf, that through Him we also may be enabled to repent. Be that as it may, the Cross ever has been, is, and always will be, the source of the great gift of repentance.

(2) This consideration of repentance in relation to the atonement has led us into deep waters. We pass to a simpler region, where the great example is plain and clear. Our Lord lived the life of constant communion with the Father. He prayed without ceasing. Yet it is unquestionable that He followed a rule and plan in the life of devotion. It was His custom to attend the synagogue on Sabbath day.[1] He was wont to "rise a great while before day"[2] in order that He might go to the lonely mountain and, without fear of interruption from the many who were coming and going, might pour out His soul to God. At great turning-points in His ministry, for example, on the eve of the ordination of the twelve,[3] he would spend the whole night in prayer to God. Living under the constant inspiration of the Holy Spirit, who is the spirit of freedom and of order, He knew that an ordered plan was the secret of perfect liberty.

Our devotional life must be a life of order and of rule. Our desire is that at all times and in every place we should be so conscious of the presence of God that the constant lifting up of the heart to God becomes a happy and natural privilege. Yet experience must have taught us that the abiding recollection of the divine presence is simply impossible unless we have rule and order in our devotions—a plan for our Eucharists, for our meditations, for our intercessions, for our thanksgivings, indeed for the whole life of communion with God.

[1] St. Luke iv. 16.　　　　[2] St. Mark i. 35.
[3] St. Luke vi. 13.

We considered in the last chapter the need of consecrating a fixed time, at the beginning of the day, for prayer and meditation. The arrangement of our time for devotion is an absolute necessity There are other points of method which are worthy of mention. Every one should make a prayer book of his own, noting special subjects for thanksgiving and intercession, writing out (it may be) some prayers which he has found to meet his need. Books of devotion are not at all to be despised, provided that we do not put too much reliance on them, to the hindrance of our own perfectly simple and natural speech with our Father. Their chief usefulness, perhaps, is to show us good methods in prayer : we may do well, for example, to put ourselves to school with Bishop Andrews, and learn from him what a wealth of inspiration is open to a priest who knows his Bible well. Moreover, such a book as "Sursum Corda" will show us what wide fields are open to our intercession and our thanksgivings.

Experience teaches us that our unhappy slackness tends to let down our devotions, and therefore our whole personal and pastoral life, to a miserably low level. We need from time to time to renew our baptismal and ordination vows, and solemnly to rededicate ourselves to God. For this purpose an annual retreat of three or four days is almost a necessity. Opportunities for such retreats are happily frequent in most dioceses. No question of "party" has anything to do with them. All priests need to find times when they may be alone with God, while the fellowship with others who are silently seeking the same renewal of spiritual life is a help to renewed fellowship with the Father of us all.

(3) *Meditation.*—We return to the example of our Lord. Certainly He had His times of retreat, which He spent in solitude. (It is worthy of notice that there is no record of our Lord praying with His

disciples.) We can have little doubt that a great part of those times of retirement was spent in listening to the Father's voice : doubtless He spoke to His Incarnate Son directly and immediately. But it is also beyond question that our Lord pondered deeply on the revelation of the Father given in the Scriptures : He knew the law, and the prophets, and the psalms through and through : in the wilderness He smites the tempter with the sharp two-edged sword of the Word of God ;[1] in the awful hour of darkness on Calvary, as well as in the last peaceful moment before He gave up His Spirit, a psalm comes naturally to His lips.[2]

We also must seek to hear the Father's voice by meditation on the revelation which He has given. Bishop Gott[3] gives an excellent definition of meditation—" It is the means by which the Bible becomes to us something almost like a sacrament of the Holy Spirit ; and its letter an outward and visible sign of an inward and spiritual grace. By meditation we assimilate the Word of God ; it resumes its breath, and we inhale through it the breath of life, till each of us becomes a living epistle, written within and without by the finger of God."

The regular and approved method of meditation is too well known to need any description here. Nor is there any call for laying down rigid rules. Different plans suit different men. What is essential is that we should prepare for meditation by an act of contrition, that we should earnestly seek the aid of the Holy Spirit (there is no prayer to Him to be compared with " Veni Creator "), and that we should try to bring every part of our mind and spirit into action : the imagination, the intellect, the affections, and the will each have their work to do. We must give ourselves plenty of

---

[1] St. Matt. iv. 4, 6, 10.
[2] St. Mark xv. 34 ; St. Luke xxiii. 46.
[3] " Parish Priest of the Town " (S.P.C.K.), p. 187.

time ; it is impossible to meditate in a hurry. And we must not be discouraged if the thoughts which come to us seem very poor and commonplace, and if our hearts are but little stirred. The more difficult our meditation is to us, the more sure will be its good fruits.

There is no subject for meditation like the Gospels. There are some Old Testament passages, and some parts of the Acts, and the Epistles, and the Revelation on which we may meditate with great profit, and of course we must not neglect them in other kinds of devotional and practical study, but for the purpose of meditation most of us find ourselves returning again and again to the Gospels. We shall find that the words and the deeds of the Lord Jesus sink into our minds, we shall see more and more how wonderful He is in His doings towards the children of men : the full beauty of His perfect character will appeal to us with a new power. Indeed, if there is any answer to the question—"How can I increase my love for our Lord?"—it is that we should meditate on Him more, until we find that He is the same in England to-day as He was in Galilee yesterday, revealing His glory as He makes His love to be known.

(4) *Intercession.*—One expression of that love is His intercession, and in His prayers for all His flock the Good Shepherd gives a clear and unmistakable lead to His under-shepherds. He prays for all, and as He knows His sheep by name He prays for each : "I have prayed for thee," he says to St. Peter, "that thy faith fail not."[1] Who can doubt that He prays for each of us now? Our imagination cannot compass it, but faith claims it and reason approves.

There is no part of our ministry which is happier or more effectual than our intercession. We may not be successful in anything else, but if we are faithful we cannot fail here. We must pray for all,

[1] St. Luke xxii. 32.

and, so far as it is possible, we must pray for each. The priest of a small parish is happy in that he can plead for every member of his flock by name. When the flock is numbered by thousands its pastor must perhaps be contented if he prays individually for his communicants, and others with whom he is brought closely into contact. In any case method is obviously needed : the persons and the causes for which the priest means to pray will have their places in his private prayer book, and will be distributed among the different days of the week.

There can be no doubt that our influence waits on our intercession. The priest who has power with his people is the priest who prays for them. The life and letters of Forbes Robinson give a signal example of the close relationship between prayer and influence. "Do you not think," he said to a priest friend who complained that he could make no headway with his people, "that you might help your people more if you spoke less about God to them, and spoke more about them to God?" How much is there in the life of an average priest of "speaking about his people to God"? Is it not just here that many of us have most miserably failed to follow the example of our Lord?

(5) *Thanksgiving.*—There is a close connection between intercession and thanksgiving. St. Paul bids us "make prayers and intercession and giving of thanks" for all men.[1] Both are closely connected with the fruits of the spirit : intercession is the natural expression of love, thanksgiving of joy—for "joy with its face towards God is thanksgiving."

Our Lord was full of joy, and His whole life overflowed with thanksgiving. We make a great mistake if we think that because our Lord is "the man of sorrows and acquainted with grief,"[2] therefore His life was spent in gloom. There was quiet happiness

---

[1] 1 Tim. ii. 1 ; *cf.* Phil. iv. 6.   [2] Isa. liii. 3.

in the home at Nazareth: there was gladness in the association with His disciples ("I thank Thee, Father, in that Thou hast hid these things from the wise and prudent and hast revealed them unto babes").[1] He rejoices in the Father's loving care and His answers to prayer ("Father, I thank Thee that Thou hast heard me").[2] There was joy blended with the agony of the Cross: "for the joy that was set before Him, He endured the cross, despising the shame";[3] the words show clearly that the writer speaks not merely of the future joy, but of the Redeemer's present joy in fulfilling His perfect work.

So it came to pass that on the blackest night in history, when the traitor went out into the darkness, and the awful mystery of the passion was already begun, Jesus "took bread and brake it and gave thanks."[4] He gave thanks for the Father's love which He was showing forth to the world: thanks for the work of redemption which He was about to accomplish: thanks for the millions who would find their true life in Him: thanks for the victory over the powers of evil already being won. Since that night the central service of Christendom, in which every offering that we make finds its consummation, and all our supplications and intercessions are gathered into one, is beyond all else the Eucharist, the thanksgiving. It surely cannot be possible for a priest in the Church of God to be an unthankful man, or to neglect the privilege of praising God.

Indeed we have cause to thank God for His great goodness to us. Even if we look at it from a lower point of view, there is no calling so full of human interest, with such openings for friendship and good-will; there is no work so splendidly worth doing. But it has the higher joy of close fellowship with our Lord in His work of saving the world—not, indeed,

[1] St. Matt. xi. 25   [2] St. John xi. 41.   [3] Heb. xii. 2.   [4] St. Luke xxii. 19; 1 Cor. xi. 23, 24.

that we are nearer to Him than our lay brethren, but that our priesthood carries with it the awful privilege and responsibility of special association with Him in the ministry of truth and grace which He has entrusted to us. Surely we shall say daily, " I thank Christ Jesus, our Lord, who hath enabled me, for that He counted me faithful, putting me into the ministry." [1]

The habit of thanksgiving will keep us continually in the sunshine. " The devil builds his nest and lays his eggs in the gloomy heart." Let us take care not to give such occasion to the adversary. There is absolutely nothing, except sin, which may not be made a subject of thanksgiving. " It is very meet, right, and our bounden duty that we should at all times and in all places give thanks " to the Giver of all good. So "the joy of the Lord shall be our strength."

[1] 1 Tim. i. 12.

Printed in Great Britain at THE DARIEN PRESS, *Edinburgh*

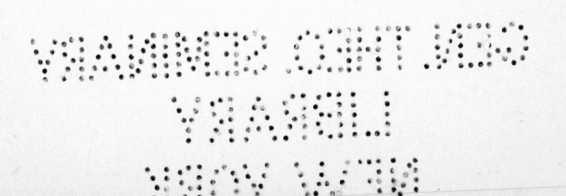